Besides spoof master Richard Armour, the iconoclastic Groucho has always been an inspiration for me. *This Horse Feathers* (1932) still, from a film which specifically satires academic life, seems an apt opening

FILM CLASSICS RECLASSIFIED:

A *SHOCKING* SPOOF OF CINEMA

By

Wes D. Gehring, Ph.D, D.D.T,

S.O.S., P.M.S., S.O.B. . . .

Robin Vincent
PUBLISHING

FILM CLASSICS RECLASSIFIED:
A *SHOCKING* SPOOF OF CINEMA
Wes D. Gehring

Robin Vincent Publishing LLC
2829 Grand Avenue
Davenport, IA 52803

©2001 Robin Vincent Publishing LLC

First Printing: 2001

Library of Congress Control Number: 2001094432

ISBN: 0-9645606-5-8

Funding for this book's paperback edition was made possible, in part, by the generous contributions of the "'Comedy Corner' Committee." Photographs for this volume came courtesy of the author's stills collection. Matt Hirons' drawings appear by permission of the artist. Frank Dobias' 1936 drawing of the Marxes is in public domain. The cover design is by the author and Ron E. Groves.

To *Richard Armour*, and the

regular readers of my books,

plus even those who are

irregular but coping . . .

BLAZING FRANKENSTEIN ...
Or, the *History of Mel – Part 1*

In the world according to
Babbling Brooks, parody is
Merely "anarchy by accident,"
Or "Jewish novocaine."

Mel reigns as the Wizard
Of *Odd* – an equal opportunity
Offender, the perfect antidote
To any vulgarity vacuum.

If Brooks had been around
To collaborate with D. W. Griffith,
American's first epic film would
Have been *Mirth of a Nation*.

Still, thanks to one scene
In *Blazing Saddles* Brooks
Had several critics calling
Him "the Farter of his country."

Dig deeper and *Blazing Saddles'*
Sideswiping of violence and
Racism show us how
Far we haven't come.

Or, chill out to Dr. Frankenstein
And his creation donning top hat
And tails to perform "Puttin'
On the Ritz," or is it "The Monster Mash?"

Think sci-fi spoofing and Mel's
Space Balls beams up ... but his
Whole oeuvre might be called
The Invasion of the GENRE Snatchers.

Wherever Brooks' time-tripping takes
Us bank on a Mel milieu in which
Things are never what they seem
And too far is just far enough.

— Wes Gehring

CONTENTS

FOREWORD

For those of us who "go to the movies" to be entertained, emersion in the font of "film criticism" can be taking baptism a step too far. In truth, we do not want to transform this artistic source of pleasure and, yes, even escapism, into an intellectual discipline. Yet, when my colleague, Wes Gehring, asked me to read *Film Classics Reclassified* and consider writing a foreword, I found myself enjoying something akin to a "born again" cinematic experience: the films reviewed took on new life and meaning, without depriving me of my layman's pleasure.

Be forewarned: you must bring to this humorous critique more than a vague awareness of film as a source of weekend entertainment. A working knowledge of the plots, preferably coated in fond memories, is a must. In fact, I suspect true students of film will find the most to savor, thanks to their prior knowledge, and even predilections. But it's for those of us who qualify as little more than "fans," for whom *Film Classics Reclassified* can be a source book of knowledge and understanding, served up with wisdom and humor.

Having said that, I eagerly commend this anthology of film criticism which, despite its humor and irrelevance, offers fascinating insight into not only the films themselves, but also the filmmakers and the social and historical contexts in which they created their masterpieces. Thus, we learn why describing *Psycho* as just a horror film would be "like describing Charles Manson and friends as another dysfunctional family." And how the anti-establishment religious perspective of Ingmar Bergman's *The Seventh Seal* owes much to the filmmaker's rebellion against a cleric father who was "sort of a Scandinavian Daddy Dearest."

But let me not deprive you of finding and savoring each morsel for yourself. They are there to be found and rolled slowly

xiii

on the tongue of enhanced awareness, in a smorgasbord of film selection to satisfy every taste. And as Mary Poppins convinced us long ago, a spoonful of sugar (humor, in this case) does help us down the medicinal qualities of serious criticism.

—Steve Bell

Steve Bell is a Professor of Telecommunications at Ball State University in Muncie, Indiana. From 1967 through 1986, he served as news correspondent and anchorman for *ABC News*. The last eleven of those years he was also news anchor on *Good Morning America*.

AUTHOR'S INTRODUCTION

"Almost nothing is known about Homer, which
explains why so much has been written about him."
—Richard Armour

I grew up reading Richard Armour's inspired spoofs of literary
gems, such as *The Classics Reclassified* (where he also documents the importance of not being educated if you want to be a
famous writer) and *American Lit Relit* (which asks the burning
question – has poetry been dead since 1882? I can't tell you;
you'll just have to buy his book.) As these tongue-firmly-in-cheek
reflections suggest, Armour peppered his parody with witty comments along related lines, giving learning a comedy coating.

As a young professor I was lucky enough to meet Armour
in 1979 at the *First International Humor Conference* in Los Angeles. Fittingly, he was receiving a lifetime achievement award –
a large silver platter (undoubtedly plated), which seemed an odd
gift for a humorist, though it could undoubtedly be pawned.

He was disarmingly pleasant to be around, which is frequently *not* the case with many prominent humorists. (Don't you
hate it when you discover your idol could've been the model for
Hannibal the Cannibal?) Armour was also a serious scholar and
he told me that he wore two outfits – cap and gown and cap and
bells. I later found out he told everyone that. But I didn't care; he
could've just given me the brush. I would have.

Parody is sometimes called *creative criticism*, though by
nobody I know. That is, to be effective at parody one must be
thoroughly versed in the subject under attack. Thus, spoofing is
the most palatable of critical approaches, offering insights through

affectionate laughter. All this is especially true of Armour's works.

Like his parody beginnings, I first found myself using the lampooning technique in my university film courses. One has to be entertaining in the classroom, or today's student waits behind your car in the parking lot with a brick (though a whack from a sock full of nickels is harder to trace). Anyway, after writing fifteen scholarly movie books, the time seemed right to follow Armour's parody tradition. Besides it had to be easier to create footnotes than to really document them.

The ten films derailed in this one-of-a-kind book were picked because . . . I like them. When you do a book you can choose your own. *Ok*, there was a certain selection plan. I culled ten certifiable classics – just ask Leonard Maltin (another classy guy in person, though not as funny as Armour). Moreover, to make it really helpful (all this is done at no extra charge to you), I've selected these watershed works from several different genres.

In each case the selection is arguably (let's not fight) the most celebrated in that genre. For instance, *the* influential horror film of all time opens the text – *Psycho*, the movie which set the shower industry back years. Plus, director Alfred Hitchcock remains one of the industry's most famous personalities, despite never having made a dinosaur film. I am confident, therefore, you will both learn and chuckle from this book and/or chuckle at learning from it. Others might have accomplished more with their lives but at least I wrote a lot of stuff down.

—Professor Wes, somewhere
off the coast of Indiana

xvi

Hitchcock getting in touch with his
feminine side (On the set of *Psycho*.)

PSYCHO

One of Hitchcock's favorite stories concerned
a man being led to the gallows who expressed
concern over the rickety construction of the trap
door, asking, "Is that thing safe?"

Hitchcock's goal therefore, was to be both darkly
comic *and* "to provide the public with beneficial
shocks [presumably, those which are not fatal]."

—Alfred Hitchcock

Thanks to *Psycho*, Alfred Hitchcock, the man who single-handedly
revived the nightlight business and made nerve medicine a growth
industry, is considered the father of the modern horror film. *Psycho*
demonstrated you need not go to Transylvania for things which
go bump in the night; you could just as easily be scared out of
your mind (such as it is) by that nice boy or girl next door.

Psycho was also called a "dirty" movie (no, not that kind)
because after Janet Leigh's unfortunate decision to take a shower,
people refused to go near running water for months.

Hitchcock himself merely thought of it as a "humorous
film," a "fun picture," which gives you some idea of why his dinner parties were never too large.[1] Repeated viewings of *Psycho*
reveal, however, some comically macabre lines – like "title character" Norman Bates observing, "Mother isn't herself today." Darn

---

[1] What Hitchcock says about the movie is actually pretty funny,
but we won't go into that here. Of course, anyone who named his
dog Philip of Magnesia, as he did, was not always a laugh riot
with whom to deal.

straight; she's stuffed and tucked away in, you should excuse the expression, the fruit cellar.[2]

Hitchcock himself had been a strict mama's boy reared with oodles of Catholic guilt. Yes, if he had been reared in another faith, say Episcopalian (which is like Catholic "Lite," with one-third the guilt), he probably would not have been as great an artist. Hitchcock later joked about the still lingering guilt which had been drummed into him as a child. For instance, when asked what his tombstone epitaph should be, he replied: "This is what we do to bad little boys." Moreover, the director's mother was the original Iron Maiden, who forever responded in the calm, measured way made famous by the French Revolution.

Anyway, as with all Hitchcock films, it is hard to get into the first few minutes, since you're too busy looking for his famous cameo appearance. But once you spot him outside blonde Leigh's place of business (Alfred had a thing for blondes; it's in all his bios), you're ready for some plot analysis. Oh, just a little analysis.

Leigh's character, Marion *Crane* (living in *Phoenix* and about to meet a psychopathic *bird* taxidermist[3]) has just stolen $40,000 from someone lower than pond scum. Thus, we can hardly hold it against her, especially since she needs it to start a new life with her financially pinched sweetie. Of course, the viewer wonders if this guy isn't completely off his nut for refusing to

---

[2] Alfred couldn't do without his sense of humor, but some scaredy cat viewers could.

[3] There is a hidden bird motif in *Psycho* – but if it's hidden, what good is it?

marry Crane merely because of a cash flow problem. This is especially so since Alfred "voyeuristic" Hitchcock has portrayed her in such a sexy manner early in the film. (Initial surveys found she had made male viewers' teeth sweat.)

The stolen money is Hitchcock's most famous example of a red herring – making something insignificant momentarily seem important. In simple language, always a rarity in film study, it jumpstarts the story. And among Hitchcock fans, which includes everyone this side of Mars, the red herring is referred to as a "MacGuffin."[4]

Crane leaves town to meet her lover and, as night falls, she drives into a terrible storm. She cannot see her hand in front of her face, not that there is much pleasure in that. The viewer who is alert to such things knows the storm is either a symbol of her internal moral dilemma over the MacGuffin (the stolen money, you putz) or a low pressure front from Kalamazoo. Regardless, storms are frightfully dramatic; just ask any meteorologist.

The film cuts to the next morning. Crane had pulled off onto the shoulder during the storm and had fallen asleep in her car. She is now awakened in the middle of nowhere by a highway patrolman the size of a Buick, wearing those irritating mirrored sunglasses and tapping on her window (more voyeurism). This is

---

[4] The term MacGuffin is allegedly derived from an old nonsense joke about two men traveling by train (Hitchcock's favorite means of transportation) in Scotland. One man notices a goofy-looking package in the overhead luggage rack and asks what it is.

"It's a MacGuffin," replies the other.

"What's that?"

"It's a contrivance for catching lions in the Scottish Highlands."

"But the Scottish Highlands don't have any lions!"

"Well, then, I guess that's no MacGuffin!"

not the most pleasant wake-up call, especially when it looks like this guy has been reared by Nazis. (If this is God's country, He can have it.) Moreover, Mount Rushmore with a badge is not only scary, he gives deadly advice, as in suggesting Crane try an area motel. In another life this was probably the same guy who directed Custer toward Little Big Horn.

Hitchcock often portrays law enforcement types as scary. According to an army of Freudian biographers, little Alfred was once locked up in the neighborhood slammer for twenty minutes on some nothing infraction, like dealing jelly doughnuts. It seems his father thought it would be an amusing way to teach the boy respect for the law. Evidently, old man Hitchcock was into dark humor, too. But I digress.[5]

Crane drives on and on. It seems her lover lives some-where on the other side of the planet. Halfway there she changes cars. One is never sure if this was a cover for her crime or if she had just worn out the first car. Was the entire Sunbelt without plane service at this time?

Facing a second night on the road, Crane decides to stop at the Bates Motel. Big mistake. Ask anyone. She must have misunderstood those Bates "half-off" signs. After registering, she has a long talk with Norman, who seems to be such a nice boy. So much for first impressions. Norman tells her: "I think we're all of us clamped in our own private traps." But little does Crane know his should have a sign over it saying, "booby hatch." He also tells her, "We all go a little mad sometimes." Unfortunately, she thought he was speaking metaphorically.

Crane soon discovers her lover's town is merely minutes away. Now, just between you and me and your favorite hiding place during thunderstorms, wouldn't you think she would jump

---

[5] Actually, digressions are a major part of academic life. Ask any *tenured* professor.

JEEZ LUISE DAD, "TOUGH LOVE" WON'T BE INVENTED FOR ANOTHER SIXTY YEARS

into her car and make tracks to her boyfriend? But no, she sticks around for some unknown reason (dare we say the good of Hitchcock's plot?)

That night as she undresses for a shower, Bates peeks at her through a hole in the wall. The picture which normally covers the hole is of Susanna and the Elders – the Biblical story of a woman overtaken in her bath by voyeurs whose passions were aroused as they spied on her.[6] You can say what you want about Hitchcock – especially now that he's dead – but the man was a terror, so to speak, on detail.

Hitchcock's voyeurism[7] here, as we join Norman in peeking through the window, will implicate the viewer in the forthcoming crime. You know, the shower murder. Must the author keep track of everything? Let's not argue.

Anyhow, the male viewer does not mind another peek at the disrobing Crane. Hitchcock has done this twice before, and nothing happened, other than hubba-hubba Crane making every male viewer's Mr. Happy take note. But this time is different. We identify with the peeking Norman, shortly before he, dressed as his mother, kills Crane. He was funny that way.

Moving to the shower scene, frequently called by film critics the most – you should pardon the expression – well-cut segment in movie history, let's be brief. Many critics are still in therapy

---

[6] This may only seem a minor point to the viewer, but the film professor who first noted this received extra merit pay and a small 7-Up.

[7] According to an unnamed source, voyeurism was Alfred's major at prep school. That and Ding Dongs. Fittingly, his anti-exercise nature was also tied to voyeurism. He once observed, "My exertion is all from the neck up. I watch." Real exercise for Hitchcock would be something like shaving . . . which, of course, necessitates more watching.

from the first time they saw it. In fact, that's why Gene Shalit's hair is the way it is today.

Film texts note the knife never actually touches Crane's body (yeah, right, tell that to my heart). The slashing effect is done through the editing. Less than a minute in length, the expensive sequence took a week to shoot, not to mention the water and towel bills. Two cameramen drowned, though actress Leigh suffered only a first-degree prune skin condition.

Part of the shock involved in the shower scene is the fact that Crane has just decided to return the money and go straight. Thus, the shower would initially seem to represent (WARNING: symbolism just ahead) a sort of cleansing or baptism . . . a new start. Plus, scary things are supposed to happen in dark, nasty places – not your cozy, warm, well-lit shower.

But knowing all these horror film rules, Hitchcock still goes ahead and knocks off Crane, with Bernard Herrmann's piercing, scream-like score necessitating local dogs be re-housebroken.[8] However, the biggest shower shock was Alfred killing off the *star* – only one-third of the way into the film, for crying out loud. That kind of thing still isn't done. You identify with her, feeling secure nothing will happen. After all, Leigh has top billing . . . and she's cute. Following this sudden exit, many viewers nearly lost meals they had had in the '50s.

Next comes the spic and span scene, where Norman comes in to discover what "Mother" has done (the silly goose still doesn't realize he periodically becomes Mother). Well, he cleans up what his other half has done, but this is one case where cleanliness is not next to Godliness, unless we're talking Old Testament God and, say, turning Lot's wife into a pillar of salt.

Now that Norman has cleaned up that nasty old bathroom

---

[8] Unfortunately, it never hit the record charts. Besides having a *killer* beat, you could dance to it, especially if you enjoyed shock therapy, or whizzing on an electric fence.

it is time for a short aside about Hitchcock's sophomoric fascination with toilets. It was just this side of "hello, perversity." He was titillated by objects connected with private bodily functions, as well as showing things on screen which the period censorship code found radically subversive. You know, like flushing a toilet – long a telltale sign of political unrest. Thus, *Psycho* was the first film in which he could showcase a working privy in all its erotic glory. And the director was as pleased as you can legally get about what polite society calls the comfort station but which, in lieu of his British citizenship, we will call the throne room. As a crapper footnote to this subject, Hitchcock's favorite gift item for special friends was the noiseless toilet, which always makes a certain statement under the Christmas tree. There is, however, no truth to the 1960s rumor that Hitchcock's favorite song was "Smoking in the Boy's Room."

Now, if you haven't made the connection that Norman is Mother Bates, there is a tendency to identify with him. Besides needing some focus character after the shower scene, Norman is sympathetic. Wouldn't you hate it if you always had to clean up after your mother's murders? Here you have had a hard day of changing sheets at the motel – not to mention stuffing birds for the office – and now you have to mop up all that blood in the next room.[9]

Viewer connection to Norman is best displayed in the next scene, where Crane's body is in the trunk of her car and the dutiful son is watching it sink into the ever-handy swamp on the back forty. Suddenly, the car stops submerging and you panic just like Norman does; it's never good to have murder evidence sticking out of your neighborhood bog. (Or at least that was the case when this project started).

---

[9] In a rare moment of sympathy for his *Psycho* audience, Hitchcock decided against shooting in color, feeling this would be too much for the viewer. Thus is recorded a rare instance of this director misreading the modern audience.

This is what can happen when cousins marry -- being afraid of chairs. Actually, it's not as dumb as it looks. But it doesn't have to be -- because it's plenty dumb. (Janet Leigh PR still for *Psycho*.)

Then the car resumes its descent and we, like Norman, can breathe easily again. Of course, one feels a bit perverse about having rooted for the sinking car, but time passes and you continue to eat your popcorn. The postscript to the scene is that unbeknownst to Norman, he has also sunk the stolen money. Crane had hidden the cash in a newspaper, which also gets placed in the trunk as more evidence of her presence which needs to be disposed of. And Alfred "red herring" Hitchcock has manipulated us once again.

He called such cinema exploitation "pure filmmaking." Translation: the man definitely liked jerking his audience around. Of course, we shouldn't feel too badly. Hitch was harder on his actors, since he knew the ultimate performance was really in his editing. Any of us could have just as effectively played Leigh's character in the shower . . . not that people would be standing in line to sub. However, Hitchcock forever denied having said, "Actors are cattle." He corrected the actual quote to: "Actors should merely be treated like cattle." Regardless, Hitchcock's direction was minimal. One of his actors explained, "If Hitchcock liked what you did, he said nothing. If he didn't, he looked like he was going to throw up."

As a sexual footnote (always a popular addition), actor Anthony Perkin's ability to play both mother and son so effectively was probably assisted by his bisexual nature. Indeed, an AC-DC sexual preference was something Alfred "repressed sexuality" Hitchcock looked for in performers. He felt they had to be part feminine and part masculine to get inside their characters. Subjectivity for him went beyond gender . . . which can be painful, not to mention being a no-no. For more information on this, or some lovely French postcards, simply phone Hollywood's favorite erotic bakery – affectionately called "Get Your Buns In Here." Operators are standing by (they cannot afford chairs).

Returning now to our normally scheduled plot synopsis, the rest of the film is about Crane's lover (who looks nothing like an ambassador[10]) and sister (Vera Miles) trying to discover what happened to her. This portion of the story is often a bit fuzzy because many of us hid under our chairs during the shower sequence and it took several days to pry us out – part fear and part all those old ju-ju-bees on the floor.

Actually, most viewers only hid under their seats for half an hour. Unfortunately, many came up just about the time the detective (Martin Balsam) was going up the steps in Norman's creepy old house. Before you could say, "You fool, you fool," there was another mess to clean up. *Psycho*'s shock scenes occur every thirty minutes, almost as methodically as Englishman Hitchcock took tea breaks. The director adds one of his dark jokes here – the "private eye" is fatally stabbed in the eye. Of course, it could have been worse; Hitchcock might have called him a "dick."

The rest of the film represents another descent, but we're not talking bog here. This one is psychological – an exploration of major fruitcake Norman, who limited himself to two personalities because he never wanted a big family. On the subject of learning more, the audience is on the fence (which is more comfortable than being under those seats). Hitchcock has been so successful at linking us to Bates, from hot-to-trot voyeurism to rooting for sinking cars, that there is a certain fear on our part that suggests maybe we're all capable of something like this.

Why does it come as no surprise that two of Hitchcock's favorite books as a youngster were *The Strange Case of Dr. Jekyll and Mr. Hyde* and *The Picture of Dorian Gray*? (You were expecting maybe *Rebecca of Sunnybrook Farm*?) Young Hitch probably did not spend an over abundance of time in the sandbox . . . unless he was burying something. Regardless, the double or dual personality theme is very important to him, especially in *Psycho*,

---

[10] The lover was played by John Gavin, friend of actor/President (redundant?) Ronald Reagan, who later appointed him Ambassador to Mexico.

where Norman via Mother Bates is (like that old gag about the excited Siamese twins) "beside himself."

Alfred further contributes to this disturbing dual personality effect as Crane's good-guy lover (Ambassador-to-be Gavin) and sicko Norman look so much alike. Thus, when they have a confrontation late in the film, facing each other across Bates' office counter, you want to shout, "Stop the projector! Let's play Twister!" (Sorry about that.) The two characters seem interchangeable, and that's scary.

While the men fight, Crane's sister goes to Norman's house – not a terribly bright idea, but it gets the old blood pressure soaring again, especially since another 30 minutes are about up. Her exploration of Norman's domain uncovers more Freudian levels than Sigmund's toolbox. Crammed with Victorian décor, the dump literally oozes sexual repression – definitely a twisted party atmosphere.

When Norman comes to the house, Crane's sister hides in the basement – another major league boner. Has this person never seen a scary movie? Downstairs she spots the seated backside of Norman's mummified mommy. But just as she starts to turn the chair (luckily it is a swivel style), Norman, dressed as murdering Ma, comes zipping down the stairs with his trusty knife.

Well, Sis throws up her arms, as you are want to do when a psychotic killer dressed as an old woman comes at you with a blade as large as a horse's leg. One of Sis's arms bumps the dangling overhead light, and its swinging casts eerie – make that downright disturbing – light in and out of Ma Bates' empty eye sockets. Sis's scream, often bolstered by the screams of chicken audience members everywhere, merges with Bernard Herrmann's ever chilling score (it's those shrieking violin strings again). But quicker than you can say "I can't handle another murder today!," Crane's lover comes to the rescue and Norman is out of the motel business.

The boringly complacent explanation by the court psychiatrist at the film's close is not so much to enlighten the viewer as to seemingly give him or her a few moments in which to get composed, put eyes back in the head, and resume normal breathing before getting up. Of course, Doc does explain why Norman did his taxidermy thing on Ma Bates. It seems Norman lost a sense of security with her death: can't live with her, can't live without her. You know, the down side of murder. Consequently, he wanted to keep her memory alive, which shows a nice spirit by Norman, though unfortunately, the timing for this change of heart was not ideal for Ma Bates.

Regardless, there is no rest for the voyeuristic audience. Just as this clinical overview starts to lull one into a sense of security, Hitchcock jerks us back to watching Norman (who has now forever become Mother) in his little padded cell. And as we play peeping tom one last time, checking out the now permanent mad stare of Mother (another Hitchcock example of death taking possession of the living), we hear her thought: "They're probably watching me now [meaning asylum security – but then again, maybe "she" knows we're tuned in, too] . . . I hope they are watching! [You got it, sweetie.]" Hitchcock then superimposes a skull on "her" face (always a comforting image) and the film closes on Crane's car being pulled from the bog. Because viewers have at sometimes invariably related to Norman, there is a tendency to feel as slimy as the swamp car.

Despite being forever spoofed, with just this side of a zillion copycat films from Hollywood, where all things are created sequel, *Psycho* continues to have the power to manipulate audiences, especially the heebie-jeebie fears which come from thinking about our own dark sides. So don't let anyone ever tell you *Psycho* is just a horror film. That would be like describing Charles Manson and friends as another dysfunctional family.[11]

---

[11] Hopefully, this has given you some new perspectives on Hitchcock's greatest film. If not, to hell with you . . .. But if you have any further questions, send a self-addressed stamped envelope to "Psycho Symbolism." It's just that easy.

"I'm tired of answering the friggin' door for Emerald City. I need a valium the size of a Buick." (Frank Morgan, a. k. a. "The Wizard," talks down to Judy Garland and company in *The Wizard of Oz.*)

> People still believe "There's no place like home,"
> which, to paraphrase Robert Benchley, proves
> why democracy can never be a success.

If redone today, *Oz*'s conclusion would probably include a high speed car chase on the Yellow Brick Road and/or some gratuitous sex (like Munchkins doing it) and violence (maybe graphic film footage of the house squishing that first witch). But musical fantasy does demand suspension of disbelief. For instance, when the Wicked Witch of the West zooms by on her souped up broomstick, no one in the audience jumps up and says, "cut the crap-ola; witches can't fly, unless they go coach like the rest of us."

Along the same lines, you just have to accept that some teenager would burst into song on the family pig lot. This is not to say it couldn't happen. But a recent random survey of people who have warbled on pig farms found "Over the Rainbow" selected only once. [1]

Like most fantasies, the key to *The Wizard of Oz* is the sense of home. Indeed, Dorothy even manages to fly to Oz in the family dump. Now while she was somewhat assisted by a tornado, it's a fitting development for the genre. [2] Another example of fantasy's forever-going-home phenomenon is that nearly ev-

---

[1] The most popular pig lot selection was the Beatles' "Help," followed by the "Oscar Meyer Wiener" song.

[2] Genre is a la-de-da French term sometimes thought to mean "Use the small fork," but when applied to film it refers to entertainment types – comedies, westerns, musicals . . . please finish this out on your own.

eryone Dorothy knew in Kansas pops up in Oz. Sure, they might be sporting a fur coat and tail or a tin jumpsuit, but they're the same folks. It's all there in the credits. (Maybe this shows it's just a small world . . . but I wouldn't want to paint it.)

While Dorothy hangs out a lot with a scarecrow, a cowardly lion, and a tin man (not recommended for children at home), the pivotal Oz characters in terms of fantasy are: the Wicked Witch (a regular bad day in Bosnia), Glinda the Good Witch, and Dorothy. [3] That is, most of these anything goes fantasies have a super villain, a super mentor, a super child, though copyright restrictions kept them from wearing tights, a cape, and a "s" on their chest. Comparing it to *Star Wars*, Glinda is a combination Ben Konobi and Yoda (though naturally her voice is higher and she's into those floating bubble entrances and exits). The Wicked Witch could be equated with Darth Vader, despite there being no known footage of him on a broom.

Of course everything revolves around Judy Garland's Dorothy. A full-bosomed and mature-looking sixteen-year-old, Judy Garland was probably not exactly what Oz author Frank Baum had in mind for his *child* hero. [4] Neither did Hollywood's resident Wicked Witch, er uh, Warlock, Louis B. Mayer – head of the studio (the one with the lion) making *The Wizard of Oz*. He originally wanted Shirley Temple for the part, but the Good Ship Lollipop girl's studio told Mayer, "In your dreams, fat boy," or words to that effect. Poor Mayer, he was only *stuck* with a soon-to-be superstar. The down side was for Judy. For a time Garland had to prance around in a blonde wig and frilly dress à la Temple. Mayer was bound and determined she should look childlike, so he

---

[3] Apologies to Toto fans.

[4] Judy had already dated Clark Gable, for crying out loud. But he was actually involved with Carole Lombard . . . and every woman this side of Central Casting. The man had needs, and obviously did give a damn.

had her bosom bound, too, or at least girdled and strapped. Plus, wanting his Dorothy to look wide-eyed and gaunt (being whirled about by a tornado often does that), he subjected Garland to alternate days of fasting. [5] The near major league boo-boo of not casting Judy is only rivaled by the initial decision that the song "Over the Rainbow" was just too darn sentimental and should be cut from the film! Yes, you heard right. Moreover, it was only reluctantly added later when the powers that be . . . make that the *dumb* powers that be, decided they didn't have time to film another number. Thank goodness for time restraints.

Like many fantasy films, *The Wizard of Oz* also functions as a coming of age movie. Just think of Judy's Dorothy as a rebel without an attitude. As Professor Marvel (and soon to be the Wizard of Oz [6]) describes Dorothy's running away: "They don't appreciate you . . . You want to see other lands – big cities, big mountains, big oceans." You'll note, however, that there's never any mention of flying monkeys . . . something that frequently makes one rethink those running away plans.

But as with many would-be rebels, Dorothy spends most of the time trying to get back home. Actually, this represents the greatest suspension of disbelief – that she would pick old fuddy-duddy black and white Kansas over Technicolor Oz – with its more than zany flora and fauna, from talking trees to those cute

---

[5] Genealogy studies now suggest Mayer was related to Simon Legree.

[6] Played by Frank Morgan, the role was originally offered to W. C. Fields, who turned it down as less than promising. So much for a great huckster recognizing a pivotal con artist role. Maybe he *did* drink too much. If he had taken the part the flying monkey sequences could have been played as an attack of the DT's. Because as he once observed, "It's hard to tell when Hollywood ends and the DT's begin."

midget munchkins. Dorothy had obviously never driven across Kansas in the summer time. It's so flat you can watch your dog run away . . . for two days. But put this question to anyone: "Would you like to vacation 'over the rainbow' in Oz's Emerald City, or be sentenced to two weeks in Topeka, Kansas?" If this is a tough decision for you, chances are, like Dorothy, you've recently been smacked in the noggin by some airborne house shutters. (Ah Kansas, where they think a good time is an extra hour of church!)

The film's most understated line, "Toto, I have a feeling we're not in Kansas anymore!" is rebelliously ironic, since at the movie's close one discovers it has been a dream and she has never left home. Don't you hate it when films end with that "it's only a dream" crap? It takes away from Dorothy's adventure. Here she has this great swashbuckling quest of a story to tell and everyone says, "yeah, yeah, you were just snoozing." Besides, a dream with that large a cast (over 9,000 in the film, honest!) would have surely short circuited most noodles, whether they were sleeping or not. And they never pulled any of this "it's only a dream" baloney on Peter Pan. [7]

In Baum's original story Oz was no dream, which also suggests this guy could really party. But if you have to have the dream cop-out close (there's always some spoilsport), there is a historical parallel of interest. The same year *The Wizard of Oz* was published (1900), Freud's *Interpretation of Dreams* appeared. [8] And since that time numerous psychiatrists, those talent scouts for mental institutions, have used *The Wizard of Oz* as a metaphor for everything from the traumas of growing up to the dangers of

---

[7] They did on *Alice in Wonderland*, however, so maybe this is some sort of fantasy sexism phenomenon.

[8] Freud didn't find a subliminal sexual motive behind all human action . . . only about 99.9 percent of them. He was also the first mental Peeping Tom.

landing your house in a new time zone.

Freud thought of the writer juggling concepts as really like a child playing with his or her toys, which just goes to show maybe it was Freud who should have been on the couch. Still, classic children's literature has as much for the adult as for the shrimp, though as Groucho reminds us, it would be a better world if the adults had to eat the spinach. Regardless, Baum's *Oz* is the reminder that the most powerful "Wizard" can end up being a fake from Omaha (cities may vary from person to person), and that we often painstakingly search for things we already have (this does not apply to lost car keys).

Baum's preface to *The Wonderful World of Oz* notes his pride in jettisoning all the basic "bloodcurdling" fairy tale stuff. And this is true to a point, since there is nothing quite so nightmarish as Lewis Carroll turning the Duchess' baby (in Alice's arms) into a pig. [9] But at the same time, *Oz* is not exactly two weeks in the country. It plays footsie with some pretty hard-core little people fears, from standard panic items like being lost to more exotic alarms such as being carried away by those flying monkeys, always guaranteed to create a bug-eyed response in the peewee set. And one cannot forget about the green-skinned Wicked Witch of the West, whose unmerciful laugh alone has been known to create puddles under the toughest of brattin' kids. [10]

Despite these knee-knocking moments, however, fantasy

---

[9] After hearing that little ditty kids have been known to stay up all night armed to the teeth and watching something safe like the Home Shopping Network.

[10] Surpringly enough, the original plan for this particular film adaptation of *Oz* was to have the nasty witch be a sexy, glamorous hooker-from-hell type, outfitted in a tight black sequined dress. Just how horny were they trying to make the audience member daddies? The director suggested this later (surprise, surprise) be dropped.

films like *Oz* are ultimately in-your-face happy. Or, as an insightful film critic once observed, "They're about the discovery of joy." [11] Characters like Dorothy who before had no meaning in their lives (besides that damn dog), now find fulfillment in the simple things, like sniffing poppies, or melting witches. [12] Consequently, *Oz* ends with the happy reunion of family and hired hands. But if remade today Dorothy would no doubt have an attitude. For instance, near the end, when the Good Witch tells the girl she always had the power to return home (that heel clicking routine), today's Dorothy just might crack, "Say what, bitch? You ran me through all this flying monkey shit for no reason. I have half a mind to drop kick your sorry butt back to Kansas. 'Over the Rainbow' my ass."

Oz's original celebrated upbeat ending is tied to the fact traditional Dorothy is just pleased, after her lawless spree, not to be serving major time in some Oz slammer. Her infractions included: wearing stolen shoes, carrying a concealed dog, melting a witch without a permit, inciting Munchkins to riot, trafficking in (or actually trafficking through) poppies, crash landing a farmhouse on a prominent citizen, appropriating apples, loitering with little people, excessive perkiness, conspiracy to swipe a broom, extorting wishes from a broken-down wizard, and repeating "There's no place like home" one time too many. Fleeing to Kansas, Dorothy was undoubtedly aware that the state did not allow extradition to Oz, or any other dreamy place. [13] Staying in Kansas was punishment enough.

---

[11] Let's just call the critic Wade Jennings, because that's his name.

[12] Of course, it was only a matter of time before something happened to the Wicked Witch, because she was obviously hyper and in-bred . . . like my cousin Stewart.

[13] There had been one extradition years before, but the accused had died in a mysterious one-house crash before ever reaching Oz authorities.

In scrutinizing films (which sounds mildly pornographic), there's a tendency to over-analyze the plot, especially among graduate students, untenured professors, and those shopping bag socialist types in the ratty raincoats who sit down front in the theatre and talk to the screen. But with *The Wizard of Oz* there is less pressure to do this, since every man, woman, and child in America, as well as most small animals (Toto has a large cult following) have seen the movie 55,000 times minimum. *Oz* is also very big abroad, especially in England where it was used in the war against Hitler. No, reels of film were not dropped on Nazis. But the British air force used "We're Off to See the Wizard" as its theme song in aerial conflict with the "1000-year Reich" . . . which only lasted twelve years. And, the English civilian population embraced "Over the Rainbow" as a future time when both the Wicked Witch and the former house painter Adolf Schicklgruber Hitler would be history.

Because of this audience familiarity with the film (some viewers even echo the dialogue as it is spoken [14]), there is no reason for a blow by blow of the scenario. While the *Oz* story line is known by everyone who can say "Toto, too," the political allegory behind Baum's whopper has largely been forgotten. Even author Aljean Harmetz's massive study of the film (over 6,000 pages on Dorothy's shoes alone) does not mention a word about this political foundation. Granted, it is fascinating to discover how many shingles there were on Dorothy's farmhouse, both before and after its crash landing on the late great Wicked Witch of the East. And who would have guessed that Toto was a non-housebroken mechanical dog forever leaving battery droppings all over *Oz*? But as *bewitching* as all this flying monkey stuff is (they were trained by the U.S. Air Force and later many served

---

[14] In such cases masking tape is an effective antidote, but if there is resistance, smacking the offenders with a sock full of nickels does the trick.

with distinction in World War II), it seems only fair to note Baum's political slant.

He was a Populist whose writings were often considered pornographic by conservatives. [15] The Populist movement was an attempt by Midwestern farmers (symbolized by the Scarecrow) to limit the crooked power of the banks, railroads, and anyone else who didn't know the lyrics to "Old McDonald Had A Farm." They were to be helped in this crusade against special interests (the Wicked Witches, naturally) by urban industrial workers (the Tin Man). Populist/Democrat William Jennings Bryan, who ran unsuccessfully for president one hundred and six times, was represented by the Cowardly Lion – someone with a big voice but no bite.

Emerald City was based upon the capital of gridlock – Washington, D.C., the City Bureauful. The seemingly all-powerful Wizard of Oz, who turns out to be only a wimp with a hot air balloon, symbolized do-nothing Republican presidents. Dorothy portrayed the perky common person out to discover truth, justice, and the Kansas way. But she and her well-meaning crowd had been taken down the yellow brick road (symbolizing America's then monetary gold standard, which didn't keep enough money in circulation for farmers). To show that gold controlled the capital (my, how some things never change), the land was called Oz – an abbreviation of the measure of gold, the ounce.

Baum left no word on who the Munchkins were supposed to be but it seems obvious they would be America's "little people." There's also nothing specific about Toto, though common sense suggests he is a classic "underdog," the sidekick every hero/heroine needs for comic relief and to help pad the story out to feature film length. (What didn't make the film was the fact that Toto had

---

[15] Of course, Baum's work was never pornography in the traditional definition of the word – bedridden literature.

a tendency to whiz on every little thing, including Munchkins!)

Baum's Populist fable even represented an early sympathetic statement about Native Americans, though the author's choice of *Oz* surrogate characters doesn't have the most progressive ring today – they were the flying monkeys. Yes, the Bureau of Indian Affairs might not really want to include that in their brochure. But before you start burning your copy of *Oz* and writing a letter to the appropriate celebrity salesperson (with Tonto's death this would be Marlon Brando), not all of the flying monkey text made it into the film. The book talks about them once being a free people and living happily with nature. White society, à la the Wicked Witch of the West, however, had imprisoned them. Luckily, fables being what they are – happy lies with a moral (everything always turns out) – Dorothy's off-the-cuff melting of the witch frees the flying monkeys.

Coupled with this, Dorothy's exit from Oz coincides with the happy ascension to power of the three stooges, who will allegedly now be using their noodles, not allowing work to deaden their emotions (they have heart), and acting as well as speaking with a big voice. And Dorothy is accorded the greatest of the rural Populist happy endings (though hardly anything to write home about): she gets to return and live permanently on a small Kansas farm . . . be still my heart. [16]

The only bit of Populist wishful thinking Baum trashed in his *Oz* fable had to do with silver. Pardon me, you say? Well, the yellow brick road gold standard was hurting the American farmer and Populists felt that increasing the silver money in circulation would alleviate this. [17] Thus, in the original *Oz* Baum had Dorothy trucking down the road in *silver* shoes, meaning . . . God

---

[16] Fittingly, Kansas was a hotbed (please, no comments) of 19th century Populist activity. Other period party states for this movement included Idaho and North Dakota.

[17] Translation: Inflation (when prices are up to no good) is more beneficial for the poor. If you still have questions, take an economics class.

24

knows what. And it seems Baum didn't have a clue either, so he had the girl lose the silver gunboats on the magic flight home. Then it becomes a moot point in the movie adaptation, because Dorothy's clodhoppers are changed from silver to ruby. [18]

The production of *Oz* was plagued by all sorts of accidents. By chance, Toto was stepped on (ouch) by one of the Wicked Witch's oversize guards, best remembered for those furry hats and their "Top 40" marching ditty – "O-Ee-Yah! Eoh-Ah!" The pooch was on the endangered species list for weeks, with his stand-in Otto (which spelled inside out equals Toto) taking over. Margaret Hamilton's ever popular lime green witch make-up caught on fire during one of those ball of flame exits, which probably contributed to the scream factor in her wicked laugh. And her smoke producing broom exploded (maybe she'd missed the 60,000 mile maintenance agreement) during a scene, injuring her stand-in, or back-up witch. [19] Several Flying Monkeys suffered bruises when their support wires snapped, which inadvertently produced a new rendition of "O-Ee-Yah! Eoh-Ah!"

The original tin man Buddy Ebsen, of later fame as Jed Clampett of *The Beverly Hillbillies*, was lost to the picture when his lungs somehow became coated with aluminum powder from his make-up and he couldn't breathe – never a good sign. M-G-M, being the compassionate studio it was . . . not, initially threat-

---

[18] If a moot point is made in a forest with no one around, would there be any sound?

[19] Ironically, in real life Garland and Hamilton were very close, while things were more strained between Judy and the four male stars (Bert Lahr, Ray Bolger, Jack Haley and Frank Morgan). It seems they were concerned about being upstaged by this innocent teen. It just goes to show one should never trust adults who wear strange costumes, especially when two of them are hunting for missing organs. (Moreover, there were lots of period jokes about the scarecrow needing more than just a heart to be happy.)

ened to fire his gray butt for being difficult. Yes, near death hardly seems an adequate excuse for not punching the time clock. But interestingly enough, when Jack Haley was signed to replace Ebsen as the tin man the make-up was changed. It seems that Haley had this contractual thing about breathing.

There were, of course, off-set problems. The most tricky to keep under wraps, given the film was being billed as the ultimate kid's movie, was that many Munchkins were extreme party animals, accent on extreme . . . and then some. We're talking fall-down drunks and bringing in regular sized "ladies" who rented by the hour. Business was so good for these working women that there were long Munchkin lines waiting for their services back at the hotel where M-G-M serviced, no, lodged the little people. This is not the most wholesome, unless we're talking "hold some," of images for one of Hollywood's then pivotal *family* studios.

Ironically, much of the problem came from big people camaraderie. Film fans bought these cute little Munchkins free drink after free drink in the hotel bar and when your body weight is not much more than a wet hummingbird, you tend to get blotto ever so quickly. The studio police were tucking in more shrimps nightly than even Snow White could have imagined. Related problems involved Munchkin knife fights over women of all sizes and missed production time, not to mention little people battling with their own imaginary flying monkeys.[20]

Whatever your focus on this film (or are you just guzzling beer on the couch in your favorite state – comatose?), period critics were not kind to *Oz*. They acted as if everyone involved with the production was wanted for some lewd act, like getting naked in front of their in-laws . . . well, besides the little people.

---

[20] While there are some who might find it more politically correct to call Munchkins "vertically challenged," I say what was good enough for Dorothy is good enough for me.

Specifically, many found it wanting in comparison to the then recent smash *Snow White and the Seven Dwarfs*. Dorothy and the Munchkins just didn't have a chance against those other little people and the original cartoon dream girl, especially with Walt Disney having already been sainted earlier in the 1930's. [21] By Academy Awards time, some recognition was forthcoming, with the nearly dropped "Over the Rainbow" receiving an Oscar for best song and Judy Garland getting a miniature statuette for her "outstanding performance as a screen juvenile. [22]

Still, years passed before *The Wizard of Oz*'s unique status was fully acknowledged. And fittingly, credit for *Oz*'s rebirth must go to a Munchkin-sized development in technology called television – what 1950s comics defined as the box they put vaudeville in when it died. (Interestingly enough, some of *Oz*'s early critical slams complained about it being recycled vaudeville.) Regardless, starting in the mid-1950s, *Oz* became an annual television event, a fantasy rite of passage for the Kool-Aid bunch, while older viewers could get affectionately maudlin (no known cure) by thinking of a past when some personal fleeting rainbow was still possible . . . before the stormy weather known as adulthood set in.

For Judy Garland fans, which includes most of the civi-

---

[21] This was a time when Disney was still best known for cartoons, instead of all the cryogenic rumors which have been circulating since the 1970 – that the late great Walt had himself freeze-dried with drawings of his favorite animation characters. One cannot help thinking Goofy would be one of these figures. Regardless, many people get some weird mental images when they hear ads for the show *Disney on Ice*.

[22] Garland had spent so much time around *Oz* midgets the easily confused Academy (average age – 106) thought they were supposed to celebrate her great performance with an Oscar the size of a shot glass.

lized world (and even parts of Trenton, New Jersey), *Oz* also holds a special poignancy, given her less than happy later life. [23] People often equate Dorothy's innocence with that of the young Garland; this can result in a good cry, if there is such a thing, and strange looks from any nearby little people, as in children, not Munchkins. So to avoid possible embarrassment, as the film comes to its moving conclusion, distract yourself with thoughts of either flying monkeys, or that old comic definition of a fantasy: a yarn told to pacify a suspicious spouse. But whatever you do, get off the couch for a while. Even if there's no place like home, people are beginning to think you don't have a life.

---

[23] According to histories of gay culture, Garland was also a "gay institution" in America, with gay bars frequently holding *Oz* nights. When she died, many of these same bars draped themselves with black mourning crepe and "Over the Rainbow" pictures. This is an equal opportunity chapter.

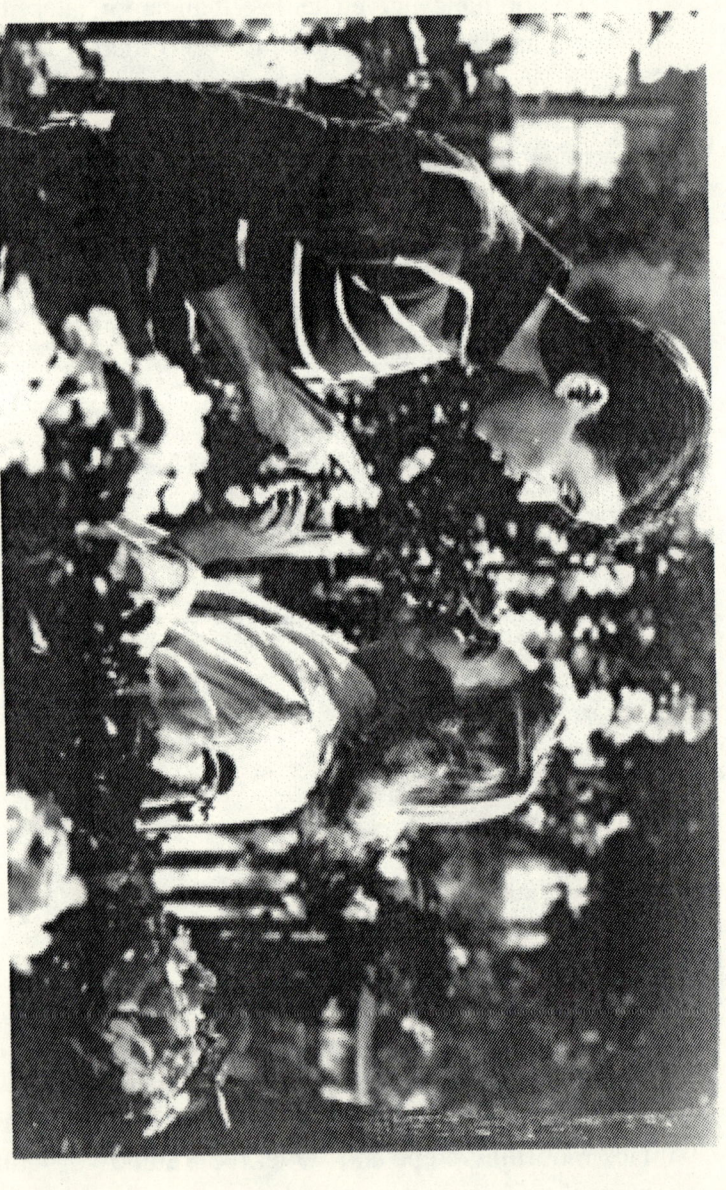

"That's okay, George. If you were happy all the time you wouldn't be human. You'd be a game show host." (Donna Reed comforts Jimmy Stewart in *It's A Wonderful Life*.)

IT'S A WONDERFUL LIFE

"Say, brainless, don't you know where coconuts
come from? . . . I'm going out exploring someday.
I'm going to have a couple harems . . ."
                                    — the young George Bailey.
After this provocative opening, the poor guy never
exits small town USA.

It's A Wonderful Life is a perennial holiday favorite, though trying
to get someone to admit that often requires finger screws and an
Indiana Jones bullwhip. It's never "in" to admit some sentimental
film turned you into maudlin mush, blanketing the immediate area
under a ton of tissues. But at Christmas time, it is hard to avoid
seeing the movie, as it plays on television about a gazillion times,
both in its original black and white and those God-awful colorized
versions which reduce art to a paint-by-number kit. [1]

   It's A Wonderful Life is about faith restored and how you
are never a failure if you have friends. (This is actually malarkey,
ask anyone, but it's a nice thought.) Moreover, the film's hero,
George Bailey, is a real peach of a guy – a regular mensch, which
is yiddish for "a real peach of a guy." George, played by Jimmy
Stewart, wrongly feels his life has been a failure (boring, a real
snoozer, yes) and now thinks suicide is the only answer. [2] How
did he come to this? George runs a building and loan company,
and one of the employees, his batty Uncle Billy (Thomas Mitchell),
has lost a large financial transaction, as well as most of his brain

---

[1] One might also term this the "dying" of film culture.

[2] Suicide is a very tricky situation; it's the last thing you should
do.

cells. This will kill the business and send George to the slammer. Thus, he figures terminating himself off the neighborhood bridge for the insurance money is the only option. (Actually, there are other options, but he's been drinking and you know how that goes.)

At this point director Frank Capra introduces the deus ex machine factor, which is Latin for the car threw a rod. Actually, it is a la-de-da way of saying some artificial means must be introduced to save an impossible situation. (You know, like peace in the Middle East). Capra's rescue answer to George's threat of suicide is to have God send down a second class angel. (Why George didn't rate a first class angel no one knows). Unfortunately, as the heavenly Joseph observes, this angel "has the I.Q. of a rabbit."[3] And not a smart rabbit either.

Before continuing with this riveting analysis a word about *It's A Wonderful Life*'s compound genre background should be noted. Now anytime you toss in a second class angel and start plotting "Christmas Carol" time-tripping (past, present, future), the term "fantasy" should spring from your lips or at least rattle around in your gray cells. George is rather like a grown-up version of Dorothy in *The Wizard of Oz*. Oh, he doesn't wear dresses, or anything (you'd remember Jimmy Stewart in a gingham skirt) but the message is still the same – "There's no place like home."

And like Dorothy, until George gains this insight he's constantly trying to exit the hometown, always dreaming of faraway places maybe not quite over the rainbow, but at least as far as Kalamazoo . . . and there were those wonderful spots pictured in

---

[3] For some reason period British censors were bent out of shape about having *second class* angels. Much was made of British hypocrisy, given their obvious class situation. But then again, maybe they just thought old George deserved the best, especially since his name has always been big with the royal family.

the *National Geographic*. [4] George is even a bit like *Oz*'s Wizard, though he does not have one of those combination big screen TV special effects machine to freak out intruders. Still with his father's sudden death, George must take over the family's savings and loan, forcing him (like the Wizard) to rule over a kingdom he'd just as soon not have. Isn't that always the way it is: people that want kingdoms never get them.

Despite these fantasy characteristics, *It's A Wonderful Life* owes more to the populist film tradition, the genre pigeonhole into which most Capra movies are placed. Populism celebrates the modest everyman figure (usually with a lot to be modest about) and credits people with being inherently good (yeah, right [5]). A classic period example, noted at no extra charge, would be Capra's *Mr. Smith Goes to Washington*, which also stars Jimmy Stewart as another true blue hero fighting moral corruption and the use of metal slugs in vending machines. In this case innocence can re-form the capital's murky (read: crooked as hell) soul . . . gee, talk about fantasy . . ..

Populism started to really play footsie with fantasy in the cynical post-WW II period, when two things occurred. Well, actually there were more than that, but this is just a short paperback. First, it became pretty obvious, unless you had a kumquat for a head, that those allegedly insightful "just folks" had screwed up big time world-wide in picking their leaders. In America there had been any number of Huey "Hello Fascism" Long types, while Hitler and Mussolini starred abroad. To demonstrate just how badly things had jumped the tracks, even prominent real life popu-

---

[4] The young George was never without this magazine. But unlike many evil-minded boys, he only enjoyed the exotic geography and not the erotic people.

[5] Capra super idealizes the people, whereas populist director John Ford usually suggests folks are good but they often need a smack up-side-the-head to get them moving in the right direction.

lists like Will Rogers had praised Mussolini well into the preceding decade. [6]

The second item that became obvious after the war was that it is hard for the traditionally capable populist hero to invent homespun maxims about hundred-megaton bombs or feel Yankee self-confidence when threatened with (you'll excuse the expression) uncontrollable fallout. For instance, as wise as populist Andy Griffith is, what could he have done if someone had nuked Mayberry? Maybe send Barney and Aunt Bee out on clean-up? Or help Opie catch some real "glow" worms? Capra acknowledges this outdatedness when the hero of *It's A Wonderful Life* survives only through divine intervention, or at least the assistance of a 293-year-old second class angel named Clarence Oddbody. (He was so old that if angels had bodily functions – our research is rather sketchy in this area – Oddbody would have been farting dust.)

George could no longer cope – planning your suicide is always an obvious give away. Consequently, by adding comic fantasy to an essentially populist film, as in *It's A Wonderful Life*, viewers didn't have to fully buy into that people-are-essentially-good-and-wise crap. They could say, "Oh we're throwing in an elderly guardian angel who's into flaming rum punch and lots of other goofy pretend stuff. Yeah, I can suspend my disbelief for ninety minutes, or as long as the popcorn holds out." Now, with smash hits like that male weepy *Field Of Dreams*, populist films seldom leave home without a wheelbarrow full of fantasy. [7]

---

[6] Maybe Will pushed that "I never met a man I didn't like" baloney too far.

[7] *Field Of Dreams* even gets a little populist in-you-face revenge for "Capracorn" cracks, since most of the movie takes place in and around an Iowa corn field that's always being mistaken for heaven.

Besides celebrating people and going steady with fantasy, populism has a thing about small town America. Initially, with George forever trying to exit his Bedford Falls Sleepy Hollow this doesn't seem to apply to *It's A Wonderful Life*. But later in the movie, Clarence lets George see what the place would have been like had he never existed – well, it ain't Bethlehem. In fact, you best stand back and put on your sterilized jumpsuit and rubber gloves, because we're talking the original Sodom and Gomorrah down by the sea, uh, make that down by the grain elevators.

Visually, no better populist depiction of the evil urban setting exists than George's nightmare run down the decadent (read sexy) streets of what is now anything but Sleepy Hollow – the cesspool which would have existed had it not been for the goodness of George "Mr. Wonderful" Bailey. Luckily except for all the potential brothels owners, George and his influence are allowed to return (it's Christmas, remember) and Bedford Falls is once again in the running for Norman Rockwell town of the year.

Another basic populist component is a work ethic that doubles for Good Samaritanism. [8] George's dinky building and loan company attempts to help the struggling poor but is always in danger of being stomped by the evil corporate banker Mr. Potter (Lionel Barrymore). [9] Boos and obscene gestures would be appropriate at this time. Without trying to be blasphemous (Don't you hate it when bad habits come so easily?), populist heroes can often be defined as Christ figures. It is particularly obvious in Capra films, especially *Mr. Smith Goes to Washington*, where the

---

[8] A sometimes quoted populist maxim is the sign on a farmer's gate: "Nothing allowed in that will interfere with work or scare the animals."

[9] Capra based the nasty man look of Mr. Potter on Grant Wood's famous portrait *American Gothic* – that stun gun satire of the heartland, with its pitchfork-toting, scary looking Iowa couple.

director throws in "little" dialogue hints like "They're crucifying him" and "thirty pieces of silver." Yeah, that Capra is subtle.

While there's nothing quite that obvious in *It's A Wonderful Life*, if you neglect to mention God is intervening on his behalf, you soon realize this George guy is too good. And one of the prayers we're able to eavesdrop on demonstrates the heavy hitters being called in on his behalf, "Joseph, Jesus and Mary. Help my friend Mr. Bailey." What, no disciples?!

Every time George is ready to exit Bedford Falls, something comes up and he invariable does the right thing. It gets old, doesn't it? Just as he is about to leave on a pre-college summer vacation in Europe his father buys the farm and George stays home to put things in order. Ok, maybe that one is legitimate, but it gets worse. When it's time for George to start college, Potter attempts to seize the savings and loan and guess who sticks around to run things? Four years pass (they're just movie years, so it doesn't take long), and his brother Harry returns from college to allegedly take over the family ball and chain, err . . . company.

Even though he went to school on George's money, Harry has his new bride tell big brother about this great opportunity Harry has to work for her daddy, who "owns a glass factory in Buffalo." Yes, there's nothing so tempting as a future blowing glass in Buffalo. George should have told her what she could go blow. At this point many audience members spontaneously begin to smack their fists into the palms of their other hands. If this were a live stage show Harry soon wouldn't be. Naturally, George lets the twit off the hook, and without even demanding Harry fork over all that past college cash and maybe simonize his car.

What you want to happen in the previous scene was some borrowing from Scorsese's *Taxi Driver*. After the rich bitch pitch from Mrs. Harry (that low life in high heels), Jimmy Stewart's George goes into DeNiro's "You talking to me?" routine and scares the living bejeebies out of her. This prompts the early return of little brother and when he asks what happened, this cues Stewart

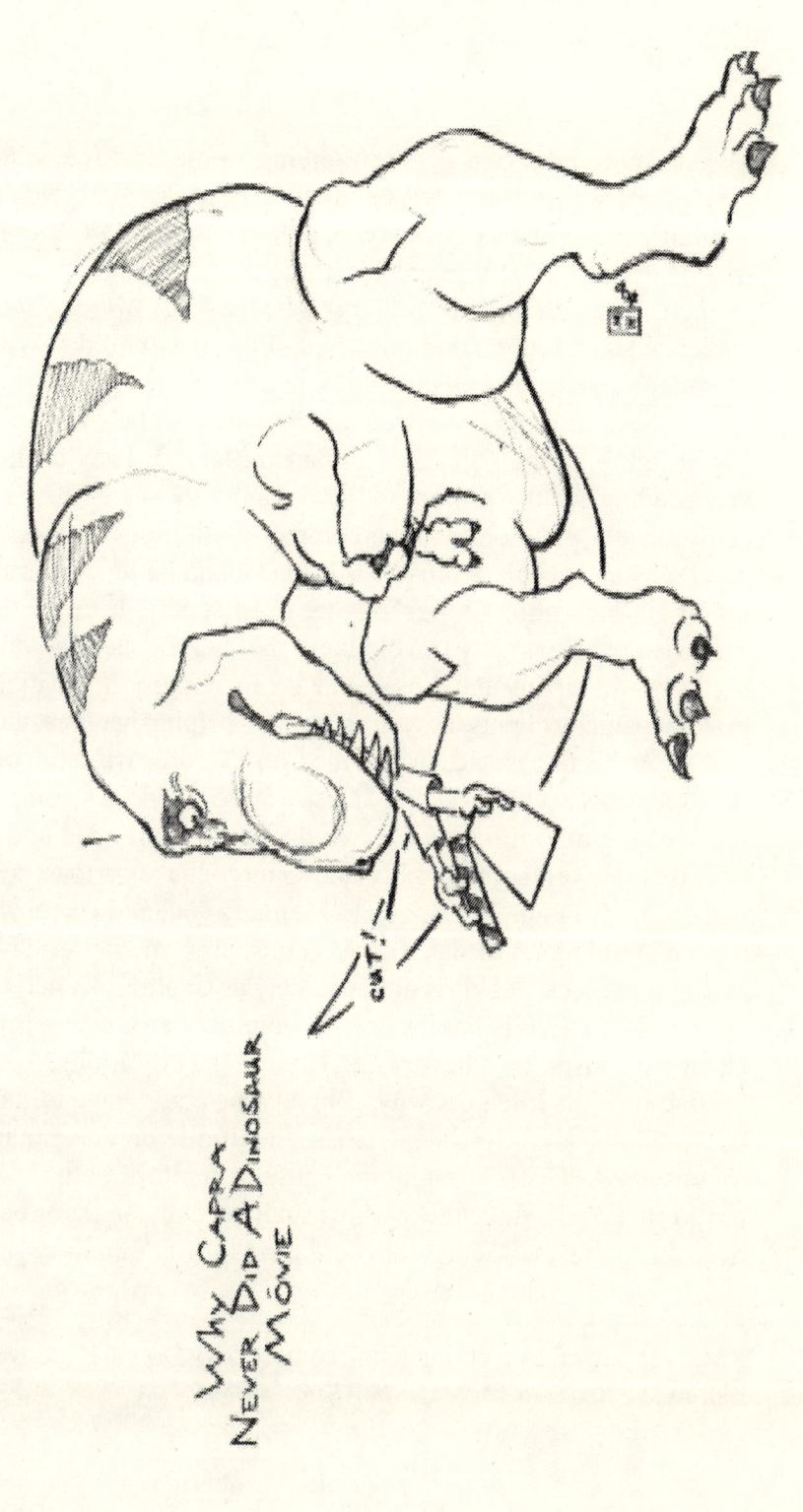

WHY CAPRA
NEVER DID A DINOSAUR
MOVIE

for one more rendition of "You talking to me?" After which, George coldcocks Harry with a monkey wrench. Yeah, yeah, it wouldn't exactly be a Capra scene, unless maybe all of George's friends democratically pitched in to help whack Harry with the wrench. Regardless, it'd certainly make the *It's A Wonderful Life* audience feel a lot better at this point. Plus, they could move on to Potter's place and coldcock him, too.

Next, it's George's wedding day. Ok, so he's not a total Christ figure, though his bride is named Mary.[10] They're in the taxi heading for the airport and honeymoon heaven when suddenly there's a run on his loan company. But does he look the other way and check out luscious bride Donna Reed (who's saying "Let's not stop, George" – that even sounds hot), or their extensive overseas sexy travel plans? N-O-O-O. He hightails it back to the company and uses all that getaway, party-down money to assist panicky clients, as well as save his helping hand business.

As his father said early in the film, "George was born old." And seemingly without much of a sex drive. George's company survives the run with a whole two dollars to spare. He and his staff then uncork some bubbly and George makes a toast to all that cash: "To Papa Dollar and to Mama Dollar, and if you want the old Building and Loan to stay in business, you better have a family real quick." This is about as sexy as Capra films get.

When WWII breaks out, George naturally wants to go. Hang patriotism, he's never been beyond the city limits, except for that time his kite got away. But anyone could have told him he wouldn't pass the physical. So, as the film's voice-over narrator observes, "George fought the battle of Bedford Falls." And he did right well, since the town was not once in danger of being overrun by Nazis. George also organizes the community scrap

---

[10] Mary is played by a young wholesomely sexy Donna Reed, years before she became TV's *Mother Knows Best*.

iron drive – always an exciting event. He serves as an air raid warden, a bit of a misnomer, since Bedford Falls is only about a *billion* miles from the front, give or take a few highway road markers. In contrast, brother Harry not only gets to see dashing foreign action as a flyer, he brings home some whoop-de-do scrap metal – the Congressional Medal of Honor, or as they say in the service, "a pat on the chest."

More time passes, but Capra refrains from showing you calendar pages blowing off in the wind. Uncle Billy loses an $8,000 building and loan deposit and naturally George will take the rap for his crazy uncle. [11] Thus, George faces one trip even he doesn't want to make – a visit to the state's big house, Potter's pokey, where the "guest" is always wrong. This is the ultimate frustration, because the charge, misappropriation of funds (ouch), would negate all his previous good works and sacrifices. And while most people would prefer folding stuff to the proverbial pat on the back, all George had was his reputation . . . plus perky Donna Reed, just a few years before she'd win an Oscar for being a hooker in *From Here to Eternity*. Count your blessings George.

As he considers suicide from the bridge, with the insurance money going to cover the lost funds, his milquetoast-looking guardian angel quite literally drops in . . . to the river below. And George, being the populist hero he is, naturally saves Clarence instead of following through on his death wish. After the rescue, as they dry out in the toll house on the bridge, Clarence is the catalyst for George's funniest lines . . . once he finds out who this little fellow is supposed to be. George, already in a major depres-

---

[11] *American Gothic* Potter finds the money and of course keeps it, with the story neither demanding its return nor laying some guilt on him for theft, as 1940s films were wont to do. Through the years this lack of retribution was the single subject on which Capra received the most mail. His fans overwhelmingly wished he had fried Potter's butt.

sion *before* he screwed up his own suicide, bitingly observes, "Well, you look about like the kind of angel I'd get. Sort of a fallen angel, aren't you." And when Clarence goes into his heavenly pitch, George tells him "Go and haunt somebody else." This is great dark side stuff from the normally goody-goody populist hero, especially with All-American Jimmy Stewart in the role. [12]

About the time George tells Clarence, "I don't know whether I like it very much being seen around with an angel without any wings," you figure hey, we've entered a new Capra-on-acid movie, but then we return to populist city, or more correctly, the Bedford Falls gone to hell sequences. Clarence shows our hero just what things would be like had George never existed. The evil Potter controls everything. George's mother has turned into a wicked witch type. [13] His brother drowned as a boy because George wasn't there to save him. His wife is an old spinster librarian. Uncle Billy is in the nut house. And the town has just generally gone to hell. We're talking major league nightmare here. George's life had made a difference, after all.

Not existing can be rather unsettling, especially around the holidays. When Clarence hocus-pocuses him back to life, George does this slap happy run through the now back-to-normal Bedford Falls. Unfortunately, when George returns to being a nice guy, the great dialogue he had as Suicide Sam disappears. The stuff he spouts as he plays track star is downright embarrassing. Things like "Merry Christmas, movie house!" and "Merry

---

[12] The shock effect is not unlike seeing the man of steel drunk in *Superman III*. Ok, it wasn't necessarily good cinema but it was an interesting idea. If only they'd had Superman fly loaded.

[13] Beulah Bondi, who played Jimmy Stewart's mother here and in six other films, was on record as saying, "I'm his mother, nobody can play his mother but me." This steamed Stewart's real ma, but we won't go into that here.

Christmas, you wonderful old Building and Loan!"[14] Yeah, I know coming back to life must be quite a rush, but you didn't see Christ making a fool out of himself. (He had, of course, much better writers, not to mention the ultimate in special effects.)

Eventually George's marathon romp brings him home; you can only say "Merry Christmas" to so many buildings. After making amends with the family (George's earlier exit on the way to his suicide had him being so mad he could have stomped bunnies), we hear the approaching sounds of a million people, or at least most of Bedford Falls. It seems word had gotten out that George needed help and everyone was bringing any available cash, from the guy at the bar who busted the juke-box and brought in more change than you want to think about, to Annie the maid digging her money out of a long, sexy black stocking.[15] Annie also has the best donation line: "I've been saving this money for a divorce, if ever I get a husband."

The most interesting contribution in the basket of cash is Clarence's copy of *Tom Sawyer*, the book he was reading when God beamed him down to help George. On the other hand (how many hands is that?), without trying to be sentimental, it is nice to have the putz angel reveal in the inscription that he finally had his wings, after a mere 200 years of trying. But more importantly, since other non-haunted people in George's drafty dump of a house acknowledge the book, this proves Clarence Oddbody actually did exist. There's no last minute cop-out, like in *The Wizard of Oz*, where everything is reduced to it's only a dream. (God, I hate that!) In fact, the film closes with George saying "Attaboy, Clarence," in reference to the angel's getting his wings.

---

[14] The film playing at the theatre is the populist *Bells of St. Mary's*, directed by Capra buddy Leo McCarey. Another Christmas movie, like *It's A Wonderful Life*, which could give you diabetes.

[15] There's something to be said for banking at home.

40

Ironically, this greatest of populist films and easily the most beloved of all Capra's classics was not a hit when it came out. Oh, audiences didn't throw tomatoes or anything, but it wasn't what people expected. It was marketed as a happy-go-lucky, pre-war Capra movie. There was no mention of little things like *suicide*, major stretches of emotional *depression*, George's frustration at *never* getting out of the burg, and an evil figure who probably trained pit bulls on the side.[16] Or, what about such non-"Capracorn" lines from the hero as - "I'm shaking the dust of this crummy little town off my feet...." Plus, having Lionel Barrymore play Potter sent another wrong message to the potential audience, since this actor had been one of Capra's most beloved figures in *You Can't Take It With You*. The pre-release publicity was of a Capra and Barrymore back together again nature. But his Potter makes the standard Dickensian villain look like Soupy Sales – as George describes him, Potter's an "old money-grubbing buzzard."

There were other box-office factors, like the winter 1946 release of the film coincided with record *Nanook of North* snowstorms and freezing temperatures. Isn't it funny how survival often plays a factor in whether or not you go out to a movie. And you know how hard it is to get a dog sled and team at the last moment. Ironically, this ultimate celebration of Christmas was not ready for general release by the holiday season.[17] This was a major marketing screw-up, like releasing an art house film during the mind-candy days of summer.

As with *The Wizard Of Oz*, it took the annual saturation

---

[16] Earlier Capra films had the heavies eventually changing, further proving the populist idea there's a little good in everyone. But not Potter; he's definitely a bad monkey.

[17] Populist films often push for a Christmas opening, since audiences are more likely to buy or at least tolerate this gooey stuff during the holidays.

effect of television to awaken a real audience for *It's A Wonderful Life* . . . that, and the message that everyone's life has made a positive difference (yeah, right), even if you never left your dump. All genres fulfill some sort of "ritualistic experience," which sounds like S and M foreplay but represents much more. [18] A love story, for example, encourages the romantic that he or she will eventually find that perfect person (just remember to have a blood test first). A "Dirty Harry" fan (never cut one of these people off for a parking space) is a law and order freak for the ultimate in "make my day" vigilante justice.

Musicals tend to encourage that need to break into song at K-Mart or the local bowling alley. Dark comedy's basic premise (and the polar opposite of populism), that people are inherently selfish and shitty and you best just steal some laughs before you're planted, plays well to cynics and others in cerebral pain. Consequently, populism's ritualistic experience celebrates the individual and traditional values – Mom, apple pie, and any six things which remind you of Jimmy Stewart. You'll laugh, you'll cry, you'll blow your nose and make noises like a Canadian goose. But if the world were a just place (whaddya nuts?), this would be its most representative genre. I'd continue some more about this goody-goody genre, but I'm expected back on planet earth.

---

[18] Of course, one wouldn't want to step on the toes of any S and M disciples, especially if that would represent a turn on.

The Seventh Seal

When Death comes for an actor hiding in a tree
(a frequent occurrence among thespians), the
performer complains he has too much yet to do.
Death replies, "Yeah, yeah. That's what they all say."

Ingmar Bergman, Swedish director of *The Seventh Seal*, is synonymous with art house movies, unless you do not enunciate properly and then people think you said "Ingrid Bergman" and expect an examination of *Casablanca* and how she could give up Bogie for that weenie she went off with on the plane.

Anyway, Bergman's *Seventh Seal* (or, if you have your Swedish dictionary handy – *Det sjunde inseglet*) put the art house movie on the map, or at least in that rundown theatre over by the college. The film is about a medieval knight (played by Max von Sydow, years before Woody Allen had the money to hire him) returning from the Crusades after ten years – he just never could get a connecting flight home. Then he runs into Death only six blocks from his castle. Talk about a crummy homecoming.

This meeting with Death is one of cinema's [1] most famous examples of the bittersweet allegory (accent on bittersweet), meaning we all eventually play chess with Death. Well, maybe not always. Some people prefer playing pinochle or parchesi with him. But these matches just do not look cerebral enough for the art house film. Moreover, image is all important at checkout time, even though it is life's last practical joke. As the saying goes, "Life's a bitch and then you die." [2] One should also keep in mind there are some things worse than Death, for instance if you have

---

[1] With artsy-fartsy stuff, *cinema* is preferred over the more plebeian *movies*.

[2] Death with dignity is not drooling, though undertakers will deny this.

DEATH TAKES
A HOLIDAY

ever spent the holidays with in-laws.

Regardless, this breathtaking experience visits everyone (some reward for living, huh?). Of course, the wardrobe for Bergman's Death leaves little sense of ambiguity. It is your basic Grim Reaper ensemble: black toga with matching cape, six hundred bucks minimum without accessories – and that's "off the rack," a condition to which Death feels especially close. He is the basic tall, dark, and scary type, with a come-hither look romantic poets never had in mind.

It is an Old World look at Death (including his playing chess), patterned upon actual paintings from the Middle Ages, which were in turn based upon very early Kodak instamatic pictures taken of Death at his vacation home on the Black Sea. In contrast, some Americans are more apt to relate to the sexy Death (young Jessica Lange) of Bob Fosse's *All That Jazz*, garbed in slinky yet deadly white. The problem in *Seventh Seal*, however, is that it is hard to get metaphysical when you are hot, especially in Sweden. (The Kinsey Report blames this on warm water currents and Anita Ekberg.)

Regardless, artists like Bergman are saying life and death are overly close, especially when Mr. Reaper turns up on your patio. The classic *Seventh Seal* example of this closeness occurs just after Death has sawed down the metaphorical tree of life with its whimpering actor.[3] Immediately upon the tree's fall a squirrel hops up onto the stump and does all those cute little movements rodents are known for – the hokey-pokey, funky chicken, and the hoochy-koochy. For the viewer it is both a funny/sad statement of life-goes-on and a commentary that comedy and tragedy are as close as life and death. Of course, for the terminated actor who has just been brought down by the ultimate critic, it was probably not a real hoot. And for Death, it was merely another 9 to 5 day,

---

[3] It's impressive that Death could even get through to the actor, since most performers only pay attention to a conversation when they're talking.

forever giving mankind its final test, though most people would just as soon take a written.

The greatest number of mainstream films address what are called lived problems: How many eyes can the Stooges poke out? Will Janet Leigh's shower scene in *Psycho* ever get to the rinse cycle? How many people will King Kong tap dance on and isn't it lucky he wasn't into breakdancing? In contrast, art house films like *The Seventh Seal* focus on raised problems, migraine stuff not always easy to visualize. For instance: Is there a God and why does He or She never write . . . not even a fax? Does life have a purpose or are we just some sort of cosmic boo-boo? When people die do their spirits go to a garage in upstate New York or do they just hang out like in all those *Topper* movies? Why, with so much suffering in the world, do people still have to cope with paper cuts? Do the aardvark and duck-billed platypus really represent God's infinite wisdom, or was there a flub in production ... perhaps being farmed out to a jobber with a sense of humor? And why do Mormons believe the Second Coming will occur in Independence, Missouri? Don't they know there isn't enough parking – or does Harry Truman continue to have clout? (To think people once said, "To err is Truman" and "I'm just mild about Harry").

The list goes on and on in the art house film, but the question remains, will you? These deep-dish topics are generally not action-oriented (Bergman filmed very few shoot outs). Thus, the director in this genre needs striking imagery, like springing Death on you in *The Seventh Seal*. Suddenly an abstract concept has grabbed your attention. Otherwise, the viewer is bored and/or pissed off – something which seldom makes for good word of mouth.

As the film opens the Knight meets Death at dawn, which is even worse than those early morning phone calls. Ironically, the Knight has always been a morning person. Still, he is remarkably composed, given the circumstances. Most people fall apart around Death. Indeed, studies have shown that no matter what your condition, Death is the worst thing for it. Knowing the Grim

Reaper enjoys chess (it was in all the papers), the Knight challenges him to a match.

Assuming Death cannot be beaten, always a safe bet, this returning Crusader plays for time in order to discover the value of life. Unfortunately, with the bubonic or black plague (Death being more partial to the latter reference) then raging, it was not a particularly up time in Europe. Plus, the Knight had seen so much pain and degradation on his decade-long crusade to the Middle East, he was desperate (one of Bergman's favorite conditions) to find something positive about life.

From the beginning much of the film is shrouded in mystery, partly from metaphysical symbolism and partly because many supporting characters wear white and the subtitles frequently wash out on their medieval drip-dry tunics. Pages of dialogue are spoken and only every 63rd pronoun is legible. But the intellectual (wishing he had not dropped out of Swedish 101 in college) can take comfort in knowing cerebrally important things are occurring, versus the poor boob still expecting *The Seventh Seal* to be a circus picture. At worst, one might liken washed out subtitles to some of Marlon Brando's early performances. You couldn't always understand him, but you knew he felt it. Well, one cannot always understand Bergman either, but rest assured he feels it.

Like many art house films, *The Seventh Seal* is a double journey, sort of a Swedish double jeopardy. The Knight metaphorically searches for a meaning to life as he physically travels the final leg (accent on final) of his trek home, from the shores of Sweden to his medieval condo somewhere in the country's interior. (And he doesn't seem to know any short cuts.)

The trip is made more entertaining for the viewer by the Knight's sidekick, Squire Jons, whose specialty is dark comedy. For instance, when the two encounter soldiers guarding a condemned witch and spreading about an awful smelling heated substance guaranteed-to-keep-away devils, horned toads, and suspicious looking barnyard animals, Jons asks about its composition. When the tasty recipe comes back – black dog bile and blood – he suggests this might just be the cause of the current plague.[4] Ok, it's not a big laugh but when your central theme is death and dying, it's appreciated.

The Knight and the Squire make for a medieval odd couple. They are reminiscent of an old Woody Allen monologue differentiating between the mind and the body. In it the mind gets to deal with the lofty concepts of humanity but the body has all the fun. Thus, the Knight agonizes over the unanswerable, while the Squire lives for the moment. For example, during their first day's journey into Sweden's hinterland the Knight prays for religious insight but Squire Jons sings a bawdy ballad about being between a "strumpet's legs."[5] Besides the obvious dark comedy conflict in topics, there is further humorous blasphemy in Jons' musical refrain: "That's the place [you know where] for me."

It reminds one of the old Sunday School song "The B-I-B-L-E," with the similar repeated verse, "That's the book for me." The belaboring of this contrast in the two men is done both to underline a medieval Christian debate on the difference between the mind/soul and the body, as well as to attract the lusting reader market. Anyway, this Christian debate has held civilization cowed for many centuries . . . seven I think, or maybe eight.

For all Jons' "agnostic earthiness" (his college major at Ball State University), he invariably does the sensitive thing. For example, while the Death-obsessed Knight attempts to get information from the accused witch about the next world (dress code, curfew, places to see), it is the Squire who recognizes that the poor young woman needs a drink of water, which he brings to her. In the course of the film this Swedish Lone Ranger also rescues a girl from rape, an actor from an angry mob (the original tough crowd), and keeps a renegade priest from robbing the dead.

---

[4] While this claim has never been verified, lab volunteers subjected to the smell were unanimous in claiming next time they would prefer the plague.

[5] A woman who has been tried and found wanton.

Jons' practical and comic nature make him rather like a Scandinavian Sancho Ponza (à la *Don Quixote*) but there's no proof the Knight and Jons ever battled any windmills.

Bawdy tunes aside, however winsome, Jons can be most articulate. When he dismounts to ask directions of a hooded reclining figure, he suddenly encounters the rotting face of a plague victim – one of those bona fide, scare-the-bejeebies-out-of-you film moments. Jons later describes the figure to the unbeknownst Knight as being "most eloquent," though "very gloomy." This is called understatement. The Squire is also a master of withering sarcasm. After the Knight convinces him they cannot free the poor witch (something having to do with being outnumbered 6,000 to 2), Jons tells one of her guards, "Why not burn her at night when the [religious] people need diversion."

Yes, whether the subject is the medieval cookout or playing chess with the Grim Reaper, *The Seventh Seal* is never more than a shaky heartbeat from life versus the forces of Death. And if you know Bergman (a tall thin man with a penchant for intellectual poses and argyle socks), it is the Church which takes it on the chin for this Death thing. The Church sponsored the lethal Crusades (largely through bake sales and bingo games) and reduced congregations to sniveling fraidy-cats by frying people alive – it's less dramatic if they are already dead.[6] (Like Detroit, starting fires was their number one sport.)

The Church encouraged the tragic parades of religious flagellations – guilty believers doing penance for the plague by whipping and beating each other, like a medieval S & M party. Indeed, the Church and Death both have a thing for black – the official color for a fate worse than life. Fittingly, on more than

---

[6] As in many Western countries where people were burned for witchcraft, a Swedish church has recently un-excommunicated several victims, as well as readmitting them to their church. The toasted people were unavailable for comment. But a church spokesperson said, "It's the start of a healing process." For whom? And so quick to act, too.

"Just think of dying as an effective way of cutting down on expenses." (Death teaches the Knight the meaning of playing for keeps in *The Seventh Seal*.)

one occasion in *The Seventh Seal*, Death masquerades as a priest. The sneakiest example occurs when the Knight thinks he is confessing to a Father and spills his guts, plus some razzle-dazzle chess moves he plans to use. This is usually the scene that most bunches viewers' panties. Death should not get to cheat, too. It's not like he doesn't have an advantage already.

Bergman's dump on organized religion is partly an outgrowth of a difficult childhood. No, he didn't have to play hopscotch with Death or anything. But his father was an overly harsh Lutheran minister, sort of a Scandinavian Daddy Dearest. For instance, a preferred punishment was to lock his son in a dark closet. Research now shows this is not an effective method of teaching Christianity, though it is still fine for developing pictures. In a better world the old closet trick would not happen. Unfortunately, it is not a better world.

As a side note, young Stan Laurel used to suffer the same dark closet punishment. But instead of going the little Bergman route of quietly pondering man's fate and how he could someday get back at his father through existentialist films, Stanley smuggled comic books, matches and a candle into his punishment closet. Go figure, though Laurel and Hardy battling Death would have been interesting, especially if they had brought along one of their dilapidated cars.

As the Knight and the Squire ride across the medieval landscape, not all is dark, though the periodic stops for chess with Death, not to mention the raging bubonic plague, tend to dampen things a bit. Still, the up side is an encounter with a performing carnival couple. He is a juggler/clown who periodically sees visions (probably caused by the elastic on his tights). [7] His wife (played by the young Bibi Andersson) is a mime/dancer so beautiful she would be any man's downfall . . . if he were lucky.

----

[7] While the juggler hasn't been able to work any visions into the act, Bergman has big things planned for this ability at film's close. And it has nothing to do with Swedish vaudeville.

These two strolling players represent the promise and continuity of mankind and provide a happy breather from all that buying the farm stuff. Thus, their costumes are more cheerful and their scenes are purposely overexposed with light (at least that's the arty cinematographer's story), viewers being advised to wear sunglasses, or at least pack them with their *Existentialism Made Easy* handbook. Your natural reaction, as a humanitarian, is: "So?"

The inclusion of such phosphorescent characters begins to make even more sense when their names are disclosed; they are Mary and Joseph. No, not the original duo; remember, this is the Middle Ages. Get with the program. Anyway, as might be expected, the couple have a young son, of whom Joseph expects great things. Unfortunately, because the juggling Joseph has dropped one too many bowling pins on his head, his fatherly vision is rather limited. [8] Joseph merely sees his son as the ultimate juggler – able to stop a ball in mid-air (baseball had not yet become a career option.)

Now, there's no denying juggling is a swell trick. Moreover, your standard Savior figure does have a certain metaphorical "juggling" ability (casting out demons and raising the dead can be a real calendar-scheduling nightmare). But the fact remains, Joseph should have had higher goals for his shrimp – like maybe turning hecklers into pillars of shit.

The Seventh Seal interludes with Joseph and Mary are full of peace and contentment toward both their child and the Knight, whom they befriend and gift with wild strawberries. [9] Such moments in the sun, sharing conversations and strawberries with ac-

---

[8] Bowling had actually not yet been invented, but all the classier stories have an anachronism or two.

[9] "Wild Strawberries" are a pivotal Bergman symbol of life, as well as an excellent source of Vitamin C. The director even went on to title his next film, after *The Seventh Seal*, *Wild Strawberries*. In the history of art house movies, no other fruit has ever had such an honor.

quaintances, are what make life endurable, if not justifiable . . . but you really have to like strawberries.

Despite Bergman's attack on organized religion, always popular with Godless critics (they cannot help it if they are products of broken homes), a living religion exists in the caring relationships of the performers and of the Knight and Squire. This is both comforting and economical, since friends do not make you tithe ten percent of your income. This modest people-make-a-difference message is the one spark of hope in an otherwise dark, no-one-gets-out-alive movie. And the simplicity of it is much more effective than a common flaw in many art house films, where some cosmic metaphysical moral is concocted – essentially an attempt to establish an alibi for the universe.

In the film-long journey to the Knight's castle three other people join him and Squire Jons. There is a village smithy so dumb that if he were ten times smarter he would still only be half-witted. (When brains were being passed out he was in another room getting something to drink.) With him is his adulterous wife, always a popular addition on a long trip, and a young woman whom the Squire rescued from being raped. [10] The Knight has promised them all sanctuary in his castle, neglecting to note Death would also be dropping in, too. Of course, while they are not aware of the Knight's ongoing chess match with Mr. Reaper, they constantly see dying along their journey.

Croaking is not a phenomenon Bergman takes lightly. Indeed, with the possible exception of Bergman's later *Cries and Whispers*, which was sort of *Hannah and Her Sisters* meets euthanasia, *The Seventh Seal* has some excruciating checkouts. Luckily, the worst one is a character you love to hate, a renegade priest who has done everyone dirty, including conning the Knight

---

[10] Jons' aid was inspired both by a chivalrous concern for the beautiful maiden and by the hope that after ten years on the Crusades, "my wife is dead by now."

into going off on the worthless Crusades so many years before. Consequently, viewers do not really applaud when he finally, as Shakespeare once said, "shuffles off this mortal coil," but there are no tears falling on people's jujubes either. [11] Some of this hostility might have been dissipated if he had had a snappy exit line, like Oscar Wilde's: "Either this wallpaper goes, or I do."

Eventually the Knight's crew camps near the castle but not before the juggler realizes his host is playing footsie with Death. And quicker than you can say "turn around the wagon" in Swedish, the young couple with those vaguely familiar names are highballing it out of there. As the Knight becomes aware of this exit he knocks over the chess pieces to distract Death from aborting their escape. It is a clumsy cover, but the Knight has been under a lot of stress. Luckily for the young family, Death is not terribly motivated (what with quotas and all) and the Knight's trick works; Joseph and Mary escape. Thus, a modest victory for life occurs at the film's *end* as Mr. Termination leads his victims in a Dance of Death (sort of a *Last Tango In Sweden*) silhouetted against an evening sky.

Some snotty critics have interpreted a fleeting Black Cloud of Death near the film's close as a symbol of the 1950s' H-bomb. [12] Not nearly so entertaining as those little whirlwinds from hell in *Ghost*, the cloud/bomb analogy seems a stretch. Now using the bubonic plague as a metaphor for 1950s' paranoia over a nuclear holocaust is another thing. It's not necessarily right but it is another thing. However, we'll leave this for some bright young Ph.D. student with several years to kill. A more acceptable symbolic "reading" (but will it play in Peoria?) would be to simply see the Knight as representing the cerebral modern individual – frequently disillusioned, both with a God whose communications

---

[11] When critiquing art house films, references to Shakespeare are strongly encouraged – it's in all the handbooks.

[12] Those critics will remain anonymous; let them write their own books.

skill seem to need polishing, and with the basic scum bucket level of so many people – except for Joseph and Mary and Jons. The little miracle (WARNING: sentimentality ahead) is that Bergman still manages to close with hope. [13]

---

[13] A bigger hat trick was that Bergman made the film for about six dollars and carfare. With Hollywood, it would be more cost-effective to simply set fire to the production money.

If Charlie had played baseball, he would have been "the player to be names later." (Chaplin as cinema's most famous figure in *The Gold Rush.*)

THE GOLD RUSH

> So many people have claimed to have given
> Chaplin his start that pioneer film historians
> were moved to suggest the original discoverers
> of Chaplin should form an association and hold a
> convention at NYC's Polo Ground stadium, if the
> seating facilities were adequate.

Charlie Chaplin's nomadic Tramp, the little fellow with the east-west feet, is considered film's most pivotal character, as well as its first 3 letter man, S-E-X. The man behind the camera did not do so poorly either. Chaplin wrote, directed, and scored all his own films. He would have done more, but he had that sexual agenda. So many film artists have tried and failed to be as multi-faceted that the phenomenon is now known as the "Chaplin Disease."[1] (Jerry Lewis is one such example, unless you're talking to a Frenchman).

The Gold Rush is Chuck's most celebrated film adventure.[2] And it is the movie he said he wanted to be remembered for. Of course, Chaplin said that after each of his films, because . . . who knew? The guy talked too much. Just watch some of his sound films. But history suggests this is the one (the silent one) he should have limited the remark to. Indeed, critics often cite it as the greatest cinema comedy of all time – which is nice, if you're into that sort of thing. Yet it's a widely known fact that critics have too much time . . . they're always going to movies. These

---

[1] This is not to be confused with people who either think they're the Tramp, or claim to see him lurking behind their patio furniture.

[2] *The Gold Rush* is also the description period critics used to describe the divorce proceedings brought by each of his first three wives.

people need a real day job. Still, in this case, they happen to be right; just ask Johnny Depp. [3]

The Gold Rush finds Charlie's Tramp shuffling northward to the turn-of-the-century Klondike, where life is hard and dangerous, not to mention without cable. Period humorists called it your basic snow picture (a genre which has not seemed to catch on), with Charlie as busy as an Eskimo trying to keep warm with a Palm Beach suit on. Ok, so period humorists weren't that funny. Thus, part of the humor involves the comic incongruity of seeing Chuck's urban misfit, complete with baggy pants, worn derby, and forever active cane, strolling around a glacier or having a run-in with a bear the size of a Mack truck.

Like fellow Englishman Alfred Hitchcock, much of Chaplin's humor is dark. For instance, the inspiration for *The Gold Rush* came to the comedian after he had read an account of the infamous Donner Party – the 19th century snowbound pioneers who turned to cannibalism for survival. Like many Victorian born people, Chaplin was ape shit over the bizarre. Granted, the tale has a certain perverse fascination, but most people coming away from it are not going to be saying, "What a great idea for a comedy! We could maybe rework *Gilligan's Island* with the Skipper as a cannibal, or just go directly to Jeffrey Dahmer sitcom – possibly calling it *Make Room for Dahmer* or *With Six You Get Eggroll*.

Of course, Chaplin had a gift for drawing humor from the macabre. He would later do comic wonders with Hitler and Nazism – not your standard knee-slapping subjects – in the film *The Great Dictator*. And in *Monsieur Verdoux* he took the true story of a French Bluebeard and turned it into the most indecently funny

---

[3] If you can't get ahold of him (he's unlisted, you know) just go see his Chaplinesque film *Benny & Joon*. Otherwise, you'll have to see a professor, and they're seldom funny.

comedy of murders on record. [4]

With this dark comedy touch, it is fitting that the most written about scene from *The Gold Rush* involves Charlie and a starving fellow prospector cooking the Tramp's boot for Thanksgiving dinner. [5] While this isn't recommended fare for most people, unless you're really into leather, there is a comic poignancy to the Tramp eating shoelaces like spaghetti, or treating a bent nail like a wishbone. However, if the only emotion you're feeling is indigestion, rest at ease – the shoe and culinary accessories were all made of licorice.

Unfortunately, the down side to the licorice scam is that Chaplin was a perfectionist who liked to shoot scenes just over six million times. Consequently, he and his fellow "starving" prospector (Mack Swain) ended up eating all the licorice in Southern California. They then went into what confectioners call the candy D.T.'s, where you imagine there are all these licorice snakes weaving around on your linoleum. Oh, Chuck and company tossed their cookies a lot, too. This is the only time on record when Chaplin literally threw up his hands (so to speak), and said, "That's good enough; I don't need this shit. I should have stuck with my chicken farm idea." [6]

In related chicken news, when the Thanksgiving Day meal of stewed boot proves less than filling for Charlie and Swain's Big

---

[4] It has been suggested that the often woman-plagued Chaplin was involved in wishful thinking when he made *Monsieur Verdox* (Working title *Lady Killer*), especially since he was mired in a very messy paternity trial during his pre-production work on the film. Need we say more?

[5] A member of the Donner Party actually cooked a moccasin for a meal, but without the right sauce it just didn't go over. At any rate, that was his story at the time.

[6] Chaplin's original Hollywood plan was to just earn enough money to buy a chicken farm and retire. Honest.

Jim McKay, the latter hallucinates that the Tramp is a giant chicken and proceeds to chase him with an ax. This is not a polite after dinner activity, though every time Big Jim comes out of his fog he always sincerely apologizes to Chuck, which shows a nice spirit. The trouble is, with nothing else to do, thoughts of hunger kept returning. Instead, the two should have distracted themselves with meaningful activities like maybe singing the ABC song backwards, ignoring nature's call, wearing their clothes inside out, dancing with a snow shovel, awarding themselves Ph.D.s . . . eventually, however, some food wanders by (another bear) and their hunger crisis is over.

We next see Charlie in a nearby mining boom town. He gravitates towards the nearest saloon with a gait that resembles that of a constipated duck trying to go two ways at once, while his tiny mustache seems more like a chocolate milk smudge than facial hair. Still, there is an air of independence in his manner, as if to say, "I've escaped starvation and being mistaken for a chicken." But then he sees the beautiful dancehall girl Georgia (Georgia Hale) and thus begins a comedy of Eros. (The male brain says, "We like women, we want women – and that's pretty much as far as we've thought.") Charlie wears his heart on his sleeve, unlike, say, comedy contemporary W. C. Fields, whose screen persona kept the ace of hearts up his sleeve.

In a famous scene of pathos, Georgia seems to smile at Chuck and walks towards him. The Tramp immediately develops an even bigger soft spot for her (his head), only to be ultimately embarrassed that Georgia's attention is directed at a man just behind him. Isn't that always the way it is? But Georgia soon uses Charlie to taunt her oversized boyfriend Jack (Malcolm Waite) when the latter character attempts to dance with her. Instead, Georgia picks for her partner the sorriest looking creature in the bar (Chuck wins, in a landslide). Not realizing what is afoot – besides the dancing – the Tramp joyfully takes Georgia in his arms. Unfortunately, his fancy footwork is marred by pants which are sliding southward, always a drawback when Fred Astaire moves are being attempted. Initially, Charlie uses his ever handy cane to hold up the britches. Then he sees a rope lying on a nearby table and quickly turns it into a belt. However, one should always check *both* ends of a rope before adding it to one's wardrobe. In this case there turns out to be a huge dog attached; we're talking Loch Ness Monster proportions. And when the obligatory cat goes by, Charlie and his new canine buddy are out of there in warp speed.

The Tramp returns only to be roughed up by Jack, who pulls Charlie's derby down over his eyes. [7] Uncorking a blind swing, the little fellow smacks a post. But as luck would have it (a rare commodity for film's original underdog), the wild punch jars the saloon's balcony clock down onto Jack's head and he drops to the floor quicker than Grandma when you kick the back of her knees. After Charlie finally manages to pop off the derby, the first thing he sees is a flattened Jack. And like the much later Inspector Clouseau, Charlie mistakenly feels quite the heroic figure.

The Tramp soon finds work babysitting a log cabin while the owner is off prospecting. It is not much of a job, but then it isn't much of a cabin. Plus, Charlie doesn't need any references. Regardless, the first day on duty Chuck hears a knock at the door. Opening up he gets a snowball in the kisser at point blank range. This is not your standard warm fuzzy but times were hard . . . and so were the snowballs. [8] The knock at the door had been from a wayward-thrown snowball, with the combatants being Georgia (gee, imagine that) and some of her saloon girlfriends. [9] Once again, Georgia's presence reduces Chuck to silly putty. It isn't a

---

[7] Why is it that the men who are most in need of a beating are always enormous?

[8] Hollywood snowballs were then made of cornflakes (ouch), salt, and flour. Yes, there's nothing like a little fiber in you snowball.

[9] Story transitions by the screen's greatest comedian seldom tax the viewer's brain cells.

pretty sight, but then an out-of-control wooer (which is also difficult to say) seldom is.

As Georgia and friends leave, he invites them to a New Year's Eve dinner. They accept rather flippantly, as Klondike saloon girls are known to do. But after their exit the overjoyed Charlie suddenly develops Steve Martin happy feet – jumping about, swinging from a beam, batting a feather pillow until it seems to be snowing, and just pleasantly running amuck. [10] The down side is he has to get work (never a high priority for someone nicknamed "The Tramp") to cover his dinner expenses. But by shoveling enough snow to qualify for hernia disability, he is able to put on a feast.

Unfortunately, Georgia didn't get the date on her computer calendar, and poor Chuck gets stiffed. Falling asleep as he waits, Charlie imagines the dinner party to be a smash, only to awaken alone at magic time (midnight New Year's Eve) to hear a real party in full swing at the nearby saloon. Don't you hate it when that happens? Well, he follows the music and briefly looks in on the happy revelers through a window.

A cazillion words have been written about this scene, and that's not even counting all the new stuff Chaplin fanatics are cranking out at this very moment – ironic, isn't it, since he is a *silent* comedian. Anyway, most critiques of this *Gold Rush* moment key on pathos, a very big word in Chaplin circles. [11] Sometimes defined as comedy turned upside down, it simply means we feel tenderness for the little twerp without slipping into bathos (which

---

[10] The scene has been much copied through the years, with the best variation occurring in Jean Vigo's classic 1930's film *Zero for Conduct* – the mere mentioning of which is guaranteed to impress people on the cocktail and pate circuit. But don't expect much response from the bowling crowd.

[11] If you're ever stuck on a Chaplin-related question, just softly say the word "pathos" and look whimsical. Extra points can be scored if you throw in a reference to Fellini, too.

is, of course, pathos misspelled), as well as being that sticky sentimentality Jerry Lewis specialized in.

Suddenly a minor miracle occurs. Georgia remembers the dinner date with Chuck and immediately goes to the cabin. Finding it empty (you have to expect that when you drag your butt in six hours late), she is moved by all his party preparations. Feeling like pond scum, Georgia writes Chuck a note: "Please forgive me for not coming. I'd like to see you and explain." This is pretty hot stuff for frequent loser at love Charlie.

Before he can arrange make-out plans with Georgia, however, Charlie runs into boot-eating companion Big Jim McKay and is literally dragged off to prospecting territory. After all, we have to live up to that *Gold Rush* title. It seems Big Jim cannot find his claim. He isn't as dumb as he looks, but he doesn't have to be. He is plenty dumb enough. In fact, his long johns have a higher IQ than he does. And his memory bank was not helped any when a claim jumper tap danced all over his head earlier in the picture. But having read the script, he knows Charlie is supposed to remember where the claim is.

Not wanting any more stewed boot, they pack enough chow for the cast of *Ben Hur*, plus six or seven other Biblical epics. After a long, grueling Klondike hike (you know how hard it is to get a taxi above the 60th parallel), the two reach the cabin of their original misadventure, presumably close to Jim's claim. They celebrate by getting a little drunk that evening, or, as the British say, "four parts pissed." Borrowing from thrill comedy filmmaker Harold *Safety Last* Lloyd, director Chaplin adds a terrible storm which blows the cabin to a nail-biting perch half over a cliff.

Waking up the next morning, with the cabin's windows frosted, Charlie and Jim are not aware of the danger, or anything else, since they're still a little stewed. Sure, when they get up the cabin seems to rock about, but hey, they figure it's your standard hangover. Both were just happy they hadn't had to "worship" at the porcelain altar the previous night. But as they move about on

The original king of thrill comedy *with time on his hands.*
(Harold Lloyd in *Safety Last.*)

opposite ends of the cabin that morning, there is a decidedly see-saw effect. Chuck decides to go outside and investigate, which is not really the best of ideas, especially with a door that tends to jam. Summoning all his strength, which is nothing to write home about, he finally bangs through only to find himself hanging over an abyss that makes the Grand Canyon look like nothing more than the part in a cheap toupee.

For a second the Tramp suffers more stress than Wylie Coyote, or Pee-Wee Herman meeting Large Marge. With better luck, however, Chuck manages to get back into the cabin. Safety is only temporary (but then again, isn't everything?), since the building continues to slip over the edge, with the slant of the floor beginning to resemble an indoor ski jump. No longer able to stand up, which is in keeping with their previous evening's activity, Charlie and Jim take turns trying to use each other as ladders to exit this wayward cabin. At the last possible second, and in the best thrill comedy tradition, both prospectors escape this early Winabago prototype as it goes over the cliff on its way to smithereensville.

Their comic survival is at the heart of our fascination with clowns. They comfort us in our short lives (well, hopefully not too short) with their resilience – both physical and spiritual. And no one better symbolizes this than Chaplin, whether it is exiting a cabin that wants to play divebomber or just the Tramp's frequent film close: shuffling down another road alone. In the latter case, even if Charlie has met defeat, before the final fadeout, he gives a little shake to his body and assumes his normal jaunty walk, as if to say, "I'm ready to take on life one more time." Not too bright but then everything in Hollywood is created sequel. Society seems most fascinated with the clown biography that reveals tragic roots . . . either that, or we are just a perverse bunch. Actually, the dark past angle plays into the resilience factor again – being able to provoke laughter despite personal sadness, or lack of morals.

Chaplin's early years read like a Dickens novel.[12] His father drank so much he made Dudley Moore's Arthur look like a teetotaler. And when it came to being nuts, his mother was the whole tree. Moreover, when there was a quasi-family unit, they were so poor even poor people didn't speak to them. Like the catalyst for *The Gold Rush*, these are not things which immediately suggest knee-slapping comedy. But Chuck's theatre of real life background is the stuff of comic legend (and the *National Enquirer*), humor's version of the phoenix. And while there was nothing quite so dramatic as Richard Pryor's comic comeback from his impressions of a cookout, what he liked to call his "trial by fire" (how's that for resilience?!), fans and critics alike have been forever fascinated with Chaplin's up-from-poverty and sexual scandal story. Interestingly enough, the Richard Pryor of the concert films is sometimes seen by critics, including Pauline Kael, as being a more recent version of Chaplin's Tramp. Scout's honor. Yeah, yeah, while Charlie was silent, Richard used every #*&/# in the book. Still, they were both street comedians whose insightful material was initially often labeled obscene. And oh yes, they each happened to be very funny, if that helps any.

Fittingly, just after Charlie and Jim escape the cabin ride to hell, they immediately find the gold claim and we next see them as fur coat-attired millionaires heading back to the States by ship. They are both happy (a suitcase full of money tends to do that). Still, Chuck is having some adjustment problems. For instance, he still wants to dive for cigar butts – something which just isn't done in the best circles. Worse than that, Charlie was not able to find Georgia before he left. Attempting to get his mind off her, he humors some bothersome reporters by dressing up in his former

---

[12] Indeed, the comedian took his first book off the market, *Charlie Chaplin's Own Story*, when critics found his life history a bit too close to *Oliver Twist*.

Tramp costume. [13]   Backing up for the news photographer, he nearly scrambles his gray matter falling down a staircase. Like the earlier snowball hitting the door, who should Chuck nearly tumble on but Georgia. Ah, it's a small world, especially in Hollywood.

The beauty of the scene, however, comes from Chuck being in his old clothes. Consequently, Georgia's overly compassionate concern for him (the woman has needs) seems genuine, rather than that of a gold digger. Indeed, she even tries to hide him, since it appears Chuck is the stowaway being sought by ship officials. Then Georgia is more than pleasantly surprised when she finds out his new status. It is always a pick-me-upper to discover your Tramp lover has come into a million big ones.

When Charlie tells the photographer Georgia will soon be Mrs. Tramp, a picture is taken of the happy couple. But Chuck, overwhelmed by hormones, cannot resist planting a kiss on Georgia just when the shot is taken. As the film closes the photographer, in a major shit fit, blames Charlie for ruining the "picture." With tongue firmly in cheek, director Chaplin had added this line in anticipation of complaining critics (whom he didn't give a rat's ass about), preferring a stereotypical Tramp ending of pathos. That is, said reviewers might suggest a happy ending ruined the film. Needless to say, Chaplin's sixth sense was seldom wrong. [14]

While the movie was well received (at the Berlin premiere the audience even forced the projectionist to repeat segments of the film!), some reviewers felt the close was too happy. [15]   Indeed, several prominent Chaplin scholars still feel this way, suggesting

---

[13] In real life Chaplin also was constantly being mobbed by newsmen, people asking the same old questions. Thus, there may be a lesson in this. And then again, maybe not.

[14] Unfortunately, his sex sense was not so accurate.

[15] Wouldn't these people be fun at a party?

that when comedy deals with generally negative situations (as in the work of little Mr. Melodrama Charlie C.), any sort of happy conclusion is not realistic and therefore not appropriate. Now one hates to be a buttinsky, because critics such as these are really no worse than a bad head cold. But many viewers find this stance abso-blooming-lutely preposterous.

Any demand for a sad ending (which the public would like to test on critics) is dangerous. It ignores the basic pattern of the comedy genre itself, which traditionally moves toward the happy close after overcoming some initial problems; it is just the opposite of tragedy (the true home of bummer endings). The very origins of comedy are tied to ancient fertility rituals (always a fun custom [16]) and rites of spring (read: more sex), events which are commensurate with rebirth, marriage, children, rotating your tires . . . the new world as symbolized by the happy ending.

The happy close is not there to impress the audience with truth or reality (seldom fun subjects anyway) but rather to give them what is desirable – an upbeat exit – before they once again enter that shitty world beyond the popcorn machine. Consequently, no matter how unlikely the Pollyannaish manipulation (has anyone actually ever seen this Pollyanna person?), it is inseparable from both comedy and the audience anticipation of this genre.

Luckily, there isn't time to get all inclusive about what these dissenting critics said. But one example is especially provocative. This scholar hypothesizes that since saloon girl heroine Georgia is most certainly a prostitute, what kind of post-happy ending can she give Charlie? Well, besides coming off as less than the most forgiving bugger, this suggests Chuck the Tramp is God's gift to women. Actually, this union would seem to have as much promise as most (dare we say some reality?) – two societal outcasts in need of some mutual love and affection.

---

[16] Ancient Roman documents also disclose that fertility rituals were great ice breakers at the original toga parties.

Whether you buy this or not, comedy criticism is murky enough without second guessing every happy fade-out. It all comes back to the aforementioned subject of resilience. We want the promise of someone rising out of the ashes . . . unless he or she looks really scary. *The Gold Rush*, from beginning to end, does just that.

Everyone is a little neurotic but sometimes nets might be in order. (Cary Grant and Katharine Hepburn in *Bringing Up Baby*.)

BRINGING UP BABY

"In moments of quiet I'm strangely drawn towards
you. But there haven't been any quiet moments."
—Cary Grant to Katharine Hepburn

In American film comedy according to Preston Sturges, men don't get smarter as they get older – they just lose their hair. In the mid-1930's a new genre arose in film based on the old boy-meets-girl formula gone helter-skelter. It presented the eccentric, woman-dominated courtship of the American rich, with the male target seldom being informed that open season had arrived. The genre was called screwball comedy, and its definitive example was *Bringing Up Baby*; a twisted romance where the heroine wears out the male with her wackiness . . . and a nine iron. Or, as Cary Grant observes early of Katharine Hepburn, "If I could think, I'd have run when I saw you." As with most of the Thurberesque men in the genre, he is less than real world capable; the guy would have trouble working a shower curtain.

Grant portrays an absentminded professor whose life's work is the reconstruction of a brontosaurus [1] skeleton, always a fun way to spend time, especially if stamp collecting isn't relieving all the sexual tension it should. Unfortunately for this professor, and for most screwball comedy males, sex is something their initial relationship does not include – a flagrantly un-American

---

[1] In these *Jurassic Park* days the scientific community, such as it is, has recently renamed the brontosaurus the apaptosaurus. It seems the good old bronto handle wasn't specific enough for them. But instead of going with this new light in the loafers sounding dinosaur, we'll stay with brontosaurus. He's already extinct, why make it any worse for him? Besides, if bronto was good enough for Cary Grant, to hell with the scientific community.

situation. For instance, when Grant expresses an interest in children (presumably rearing them, as opposed to W. C. Fields' desire to have them par-boiled), the professor's fiancée (Virginia Walker) tells him nothing must interfere with his work. Then gesturing towards the giant brontosaurus skeleton she says, "This will be our child." A truly scary concept, especially when you figure in the cost of new shoes for a brontosaurus, not to mention when "junior" needs braces and a new bike. And this says nothing about getting him to stay in time-out.

Despite the fiancée's totally wacked out concept of family life, the skeleton does represent an excellent metaphor for both Grant's sex life and career – dead as a doorknob. So what he needs is a jump-start from a real woman, as in Hepburn. And just in case you missed the *dead* dinosaur analogy, Katharine hangs out with a very much *alive* leopard named Baby. Thus, time with Kate promises to be uplifting. In fact, critics have sometimes suggested that the duo's search for Grant's missing intercoastal clavicle (that's a dinosaur bone to you) is really a hunt for Cary's manhood (read *private* parts).

The later loose remake of the film, *What's Up Doc?* would seem to bear this out, since the absentminded professor here (Ryan O'Neal) is missing his *rocks*. This 1970s version practically creates a cottage industry devoted to double entendres about finding them. For example, O'Neal is a musicologist who frequently finds it necessary to play his rocks – an interesting situation since he's definitely not getting any . . . romantic input with his strait-*laced* fiancée.

Grant and Hepburn first meet on a golf course in *Bringing Up Baby*, and it's war at first sight. She begins by smacking his golf ball and then swiping his car. All the weirdness anyone could want is available in her surrealistic courtship tendencies, sort of a cross between the Katzenjammer Kids and Attila the Hun. Grant is her romantic prey and on this subject she has a one-track mind, though there seem to be weeds growing over the tracks. Yes, unlike other period Hepburn classics, such as *The Philadelphia Story*, where she played the ice goddess in need of thawing, in *Bringing Up Baby* she is simply a major loon.[2] And that's quite an accomplishment when you figure the standard screwball comedy cast could pass for a talent show at a mental institution. Then again, as with any asylum, all you need is an empty room and the right kind of people.

While the screwball hero is a major putz and tries to be logical in a booby hatch world, the heroine just goes with the crazy flow. It's like she is a student of medical science and the principle behind vaccine. You know, you don't want to get a certain disease, so you get a shot of serum into your body that contains some of that disease. Pardon me? That always sounds a little N-U-T-S! But in the world of screwball comedy "nuts" is just what the doctor ordered. And every screwball heroine worth her loony bin documentation has seemingly been inoculated with enough silly serum to take on this bedlam world in the best of Mad Hatter traditions. Period baseball star Ted Williams might have been describing the screwball genre when he said, "If you don't think too well, don't think too much."

Part of this movie craziness reflected the times. Screwball comedy was born during the 1930s depression, when so many people were jumping off roofs they had to take numbers. If Dickens had written *A Tale of Two Cities* during the depression he would have simply said, "It was the worst of times . . . period!" It was an hour in which the system no longer seemed to work, and a genre based in absurdity was more than timely. Yet screwball comedy provided la-de-da escapism. There were no breadlines in these

---

[2] Even the Spencer Tracy-Katherine Hepburn films were born of the ice goddess tradition – i.e., *Woman of the Year*. It's as if they were drawing from the first real encounter of the performers, where Hepburn notes she's taller and a common friend observes, "It won't take him long to cut you down to size."

films, just a lifestyle to die for.

Even if you are philosophically opposed to wealth (really?), you shouldn't let it get around, because you might change your mind if someone offered you a stack of money. Regardless, the most eccentric of beautiful people are then dropped into this setting (probably on their heads, given their increasingly zany behavior). If there was a television program about the genre it would best be called, *Lifestyles of the Rich and Crazy*.

The low income viewer (selling pencils on the '30s street corner only brought in so much) could still feel superior to these wealthy candidates for a padded room. [3]   That is, it's better to be poor than to be off your nut . . . whatever your bank account. [4] Marxist period critics (disciples of Karl, not Groucho) saw the whole screwball genre as a capitalist conspiracy orchestrated by the White House. Yeah, right, as if President Roosevelt could even control Eleanor, let alone Hollywood. It makes about as much sense as another crackers '30s film rumor, that Shirley Temple was really an adult midget informant for the government – presumably gathering information between numbers with Bill "Bojangles" Robinson.

Still, these Commie critics did get one thing right; screwball comedies were "implosive." No, that doesn't mean to literally burst inward (that was being saved for the horror film). But you do get credit for raising your hand and attempting an answer. Implosive here means pulling together different social classes, such as *Bringing Up Baby*'s coupling of stinking rich Hepburn with

---

[3] The '30s term for this out-to-lunch behavior was being "pixilated," sort of a cross between D.T.'s and that frozen headache you get when you eat your ice cream too quickly.

[4] This is, of course, bullshit. Study after study shows that among people who have been both rich and poor, rich was better. And this was one study in which there was no margin of error. So let's have no more talk about it, please.

poor professor (redundant) Grant. Obviously, the Commies wanted an *explosion* between the classes, not this implosive "Kum Ba Ya" crap.

Besides the escapist attraction of this genre (one might note Julia Roberts' more recent Rodeo Drive charge card fantasy scenes from *Pretty Woman*), screwball comedy manages to be sexy without sex (damn). This is also a product of the 1930s. The genre surfaced shortly after the Catholic Legion of Decency (a '30s Moral Majority, with ties to every Holy Roller this side of Father Flanagan) forced Hollywood to censor its movies – never a fun development. Among the blue nose decrees from the new Hays Office (which tried to root out evil with no's) was that kisses were about as hot as it could get – and don't even think about any tongue. Predictably, if a couple was ever briefly horizontal, each individual had to keep at least one foot on the floor at all times (honest!). Thus, even if some sexy leeway had been granted, with the floor ruling a couple would have to be contortionists to get lucky, and then they'd probably need major medical to recover.

More recent scholarship timidly suggests between the lines (untenured professors are cowardly by nature) that the booby hatch activities of screwball comedy characters might just be caused by all that repressed sexuality – never a pretty sight. Whether you believe Hepburn's crackers behavior in *Bringing Up Baby* was a product of her being so horny she could explode (none of that "implosion" stuff here), sex makes for more provocative reading than the standard academic twaddle. And underlining seems to come so much easier.

The first sexy bit in *Bringing Up Baby* occurs just after the golf scene, where Hepburn has swiped everything of Grant's this side of his Fruit of the Looms. Appropriately, she then drives away with him still on the car's running board. They happen to meet again that evening in a nightclub, where they accidentally rip each other's clothing. Yes, torn clothing is always a good indicator that something sexy is on the way. In this case, Hepburn's lovely, long-legged backside and panties are exposed and Grant, ever the gentleman, must try to cover all this up . . . work, work, work.

He goes from several suggestive plantings of his top hat on her keister, to buddying up behind her (at Hepburn's request). She asks him to get closer so often that one half expects Grant to quote the Groucho line from a similar situation: "If I were any closer, I'd be in front of you."[5] When they're meshed as erotically tightly as possible (the things we do for friends with exposed underwear), they exit the nightclub in a precise quick lock step that manages to be both humorous and hot.

How this got by the censorship office is anyone's guess, though Grant and Hepburn do keep their feet on the ground at all times. It's that rare example of the Hays Office, rather than the movies, being compromised.[6] Actually, the scene might have been even racier. It was inspired by a provocative real-life incident that happened to Grant. It seems the actor was in a theatre balcony and as he stood to let a woman pass he couldn't help noticing his fly was down (though it might have been the breeze). As he zipped his fly shut he caught her frock in it. Yeah, right. Anyway, Grant and the zipper lady had to perform a tight lock step to the theatre manager's office where a delicate operation (we're talking the fly of a major star here) with a pair of pliers (ouch) took place between the zipper and a wayward dress.

The hasty but erotic exit of Grant and Hepburn caused the professor to miss an important dinner date with Mr. Peabody (George Irving), the lawyer for a potential fat cat donor to the

---

[5] One might also paraphrase a Robert Benchley comment on a related situation – any closer and it would have been adultery.

[6] A period underground ditty about the Hays Office was called "Stop, Look, and Less Sin."

professor's work – the ever popular reassembling of Jurassic Age bones. [7] Ironically, during the duo's tour-de-silly exit Grant acknowledges the entering lawyer with, "I'll be with you in a minute, Mr. Peabody," something Hepburn's "assistance" causes him to repeat numerous times during the movie but never accomplish.

Hepburn claims to know Peabody, whom she calls Boopie, not a good sign. She then offers to take Grant to Boopie's home. (Always be wary of assistance from *crazy* people.) By the time they arrive it's late, because Hepburn has driven them there by way of China. (Remember, she has already picked out the unsuspecting Grant as her future stud muffin, once she reactivates him, so to speak.) Still, she cannot believe anyone would be in bed. Grant responds, "If they expected a visit from you they could [be in bed], and pull the covers over their head." Evidently Boopie anticipated them, because he was in bed, though there was never any indication of just how high the covers were.

Fortunately, Hepburn knows the location of Peabody's bedroom (which might also explain where that Boopie nickname comes from – but then again, one shouldn't cast aspersions without photos). When Grant and Hepburn arrive under Peabody's second story window, she throws some small pebbles against the panes. When this does not seem to awaken him, she unearths a rock of better than baseball proportions and launches it towards the window with Nolan Ryan speed. As luck would have it, though not for Peabody, it is precisely at this moment that he steps out on the balcony and gets brained.

Grant and Hepburn then exit the Peabody estate quicker than you can say hit and run. But of course Boopie survives; like

---

[7] On those rare occasions when a job reared its ugly head in screwball comedy, it was invariably one middle America found ever so questionable . . . like running down brontosaurus parts during the Depression.

78

a Tom and Jerry cartoon, nobody gets hurt in screwball comedy. However, Grant tells Hepburn that in the future he'd prefer seeing "Mr. Peabody alone and unarmed." Despite this attempted break with Mad Hatter Hepburn, Grant's next day phone conversation with his fiancée already has him sounding like prime loony bin material: "I did see him [Boopie] but I didn't see him. I spoke to him but I didn't speak to him."

Immediately after Grant spouts this gibberish (luckily he has university tenure [8]), Hepburn calls and begins phase one of kidnapping him to the country. The title character, Baby the leopard, has just arrived in her possession and she pretends the animal is having her for lunch to scare Grant into rushing over to save her. [9] The ploy works (was there ever any doubt?) and Grant soon finds himself helping Hepburn take Baby to her aunt's estate in rural Connecticut. On the way a minor fender bender with a truck full of chickens and ducks helps the plot along in two ways, besides giving Baby a between-meal snack.

First, it reveals that when the leopard is upset (they didn't let him eat all the birds) he can only be controlled by a chorus of "I Can't Give You Anything But Love" (you have to expect this kind of thing in screwball comedy.) [10] Second, the feathers-everywhere accident leaves Grant looking like an oversized Henny Penny and necessitates that he clean up at the estate, which in turn allows Hepburn to get rid of his clothes. Besides helping her control him, it is also the catalyst for the film's funniest scene. After his shower and desperate for anything to wear, he puts on

---

[8] Tenure means never having to say you're sorry.

[9] Feminists are divided on the screwball heroine. Many like her because she makes the male seem as dumb as a post. But other feminists would just as soon have root canal work, since the woman is still just chasing a damn man, as opposed to changing the world, or at least her own oil.

[10] Neither Grant nor Hepburn could carry a tune with two hands.

Hepburn's frilly bathrobe. He suddenly confronts Aunt Elizabeth (May Robson), who asks why he is dressed that way. His response is to yell, "Because I just went *gay* all of a sudden" and to leap high in the air as if he'd been goosed.

Laughter from Grant's gay comment can even be hazardous to your health. A pregnant woman attending a revival of the film several years ago in Venice, California, laughed so hard at this scene she went into labor early. Thus, if you're as densely populated as she was, or if the timing isn't what it should be on your pacemaker, you might avoid this scene, or at least get a grip on yourself before it starts. You've been duly warned.

In the 1930s homosexuals were not commonly referred to as gays, though *Bringing Up Baby* director Howard Hawks might still have been going for this meaning, since he tended to place his screwball comedy men in sexually ambiguous situations. We're talking dresses, lacy bath robes, wigs . . . the whole nine yards. [11] It is as if Hawks were spoofing his overly macho, dripping-with-masculinity action heroes, such as James "Mr. Testosterone" Cagney in *The Crowd Roars* and *Ceiling Zero*. Compared to Cagney, even the Marlboro Man is a sissy. In a related sideswiping of gender norms, Hawks suggested elitist director Joseph von Sternberg have Marlene Dietrich both dress as a man and kiss another woman in *Morocco*. [12] Hawks was either into the inherent comic and dramatic tension (read kinkiness) of gender ambiguity, or he *skipped* to a different drummer. But he made it look Astaire easy.

Regardless, by the time Grant reached Aunt Elizabeth's,

----

[11] There is, however, no hard evidence that J. Edgar Hoover ever auditioned for a Hawks comedy.

[12] Though von Sternberg encouraged the belief he was from Vienna, he really hailed from Brooklyn, having gifted himself with the "von."

whether covered in chicken feathers, or jumping about in the most feminine of robes, he is finally becoming wary of Hepburn: "The only way you'll ever get me to follow another of your suggestions is to hold a bright object in front of my eyes and twirl it." Tough talk is never quite as impressive, however, when you look as though you are molting. Plus, several new developments scramble Grant's resolve. The real knee-buckler is the search for his intercoastal clavicle – you know, the bronto bone that symbolizes Grant's long dead Mr. Happy.

Naturally, Hepburn is there to help. While it took three expeditions five years to find the bone in the first place, Aunt Elizabeth's dog George buries it somewhere in under two minutes. [13] Now Grant and Hepburn need only search a 26-acre estate! They stop and dig whenever George stops and digs but like a Thurber dog, he seems as crackers as they are. Professor Grant is the most bent out of shape, given this is his longest sustained exposure to the real world (if Connecticut qualifies).

Hepburn, whose main goal is jumping *all* of Grant's bones, eventually comes up with a patented screwball heroine suggestion: "Now that they [the expeditions] know where to find them, couldn't you just send them back to get another?" This is one of those moments where our mild-mannered professor momentarily seems to be auditioning for the Jekyll to Hyde transition scene. But it passes, and screwball comedy *does not* experience its first bludgeoning of a heroine with a shovel.

While it would seem that Hepburn and Grant have about as much chance for happiness as ducks in the desert, the story soon places them in a bonding situation . . . well, if not bonding, at least (with one exception) less likely to do bodily harm to each

---

[13] George is played by the wirehaired terrier Asta, the most famous '30s movie pooch this side of Toto. Hollywood even gave him a special little canine Oscar. Honest. Things this silly you just cannot make up.

other. They begin a trek into the forests of Connecticut (don't cancel your reservations to Yosemite) in search of runaways George and Baby. Naturally, they are armed with standard big game hunting weapons, such as croquet mallets and butterfly nets. [14]

For Grant there's probably a kind of freedom in already being so screwed; things can't get any worse . . . he thinks. But midway through the Connecticut woods he takes an epic fall, only to be further squashed by a falling Hepburn, who tops off his klutz-cum-hero feelings by snaring his head with her butterfly net. At this point Grant nearly loses it. He gets this look in his eyes that is just . . . scary. You can almost see the meltdown going on in his head. It's a good example of why there should be restrictions on handgun ownership. Yet, Grant soon learns to depend upon Hepburn . . . after she accidentally pulverizes his glasses. Of course, the things he has been doing since teaming with her he could have done just as well with his eyes closed, anyway.

Regardless, their sojourn (do you think that word's too much?) into the woods has sometimes been compared to the enchanted forest of Shakespeare's *A Midsummer Night's Dream*. Unfortunately, when some artsy-fartsy academics go slumming in film they have to elevate their mere popular culture subject. But in *Dream* it is the mischievous sprite Puck, through magic and mistake, who creates a musical chair romance, and it is his magic which corrects things. The couples remain innocent (at least that's their story) and they revert to normal (such as it is) when Puck lightens up.

In contrast, there is nothing innocent about Hepburn, nor any other screwball comedy heroine. These women are dangerous and should be watched carefully. They're the kind of loons

---

[14] The gag line within the film about what to take to catch a leopard is . . . "a bigger leopard."

who could have first seen the potential for making glue out of horses, so never turn your back on one of them. And unlike *Dream*, no one in *Bringing Up Baby* comes out of their screwball spell – they're nuts from beginning to end. Plus, Shakespeare had no man-eating leopard in his forests (16th century budgets being what they were), so the thrill comedy of being devoured with your sweetie has always been decidedly missing in his work.

Speaking of leopards (note the smooth transition), *Bringing Up Baby* introduces a second leopard in the forest segment. Unlike Hepburn's tame animal, however, the second one is an escaped carnival cat who is wanted for grazing on a trainer. Naturally, much of the resulting scare comedy is drawn from characters mistaking the killer leopard with good old reliable, housebroken, "I Can't Give You Anything But Love" Baby. Fittingly, it is Hepburn, the most fearless cast member when it came to working with the cats, who brings in the dangerous leopard near the film's close. In contrast, Grant's real life fear of leopards (which sounds perfectly reasonable), what medical science clinically terms "debilitating heebie-jeebies," compliments his *Bringing Up Baby* character, who faints after encountering one. [15]

The last large cast scene of the film finds them all jailed for charges ranging from theft to not having all their buttons. Hepburn feels they'll soon get out once the authorities discover who they are. Grant counters, "When they find out who you are, they'll pad the cell." Recognizing the truth in this (screwball heroines seldom recognize anything but their own autonomy), she es-

---

[15] During the film' production Hepburn raised Grant's ire (which sounds suggestive but is perfectly acceptable in Hollywood) by dropping a fake leopard through the top of his dressing room. This was one of those rare instances when Mr. Calm and Collected let out such a yell that many area dogs had to be rehousebroken.

capes. But this is only a minor accomplishment, since her two jailers make Laurel and Hardy look like rocket scientists. She soon returns with the killer cat and things are eventually sorted out, after the cast initially runs away from the leopard.

The movie closes as it began (ah, the symmetry of art), with Grant working on his giant brontosaurus skeleton. Only this time, Hepburn comes charging in with the missing intercoastal clavicle. And naturally she wants to put it in (wink, wink). But Grant, being no dummy despite that glassy-eyed, absentminded professor puss, is still scared of Hepburn and he highballs it up a ladder to hide in the scaffolding behind his dinosaur child . . . so to speak. His expression is that of a man who, after being flattened by a Mack Truck, looks up to see the thing backing up to have another go at him.

Hepburn follows, loses her balance, and inadvertently mounts said brontosaurus. Well, dinosaur skeletons are either not as strong as they used to be, or Hepburn had gained some weight since her leopard hunting days. The whole thing collapses quicker than you can say good-bye research grant. Grant just manages to save Hepburn and pull her up on the scaffolding. And at this point he either recognizes his opposites-*attract* (Hepburn would spell it *attack*) love for her, or he is merely worn down to a capitulation. As Streisand's character says at the conclusion of the *What's Up, Doc?* remake, "You can't fight a tidal wave."

Some critics contest the realism of Grant accepting her after she sends his brontosaurus to smithereensville. But besides the man having obvious needs, where's the logic in applying realism to a *screwball* genre? Moreover, she has saved him from the no fun rigidity which threatens all screwball comedy males. And what better metaphor is there than a dinosaur pratfall to symbolize the freeing spirit of the genre?

So the next time you meet some dissenting academic, slap him around a bit. You'll feel better and, who knows, you just might save him from some rigidity, too. Unless you put him in traction.

> *Chinatown* director Roman Polanski said, "When
> people leave the theatre, they shouldn't be allowed
> to think that everything is all right with the world.
> It isn't. And very little in life has a nice ending." I
> believe it was also at this time that he said, "Don't
> you hate happy people. You just know they don't
> have all the facts."

Polanski's *Chinatown* is one of the pivotal film noir works. "Film noir" is French for "life sucks," or "why me?" It is about the dark side of the American dream, like when you find out the pillar of the community has a thing about sheep, or the local Girl Scout leader is dealing hashish (screw the cookies [1]). The central noir character in *Chinatown* is a tough guy detective, played by Jack Nicholson before he slipped into his over-the-top, hello psychotic acting style. Thus, it is a restrained characterization in the old Sam Spade – Philip Marlowe tradition, though you might just as well say Humphrey Bogart, since he forever screwed up differentiating between the two by playing both in the movies.

The film noir dick (that's detective to you) is not overly bright, or else he wouldn't be getting smacked over the head every six minutes. He doesn't figure the mystery out any faster than the viewer, despite having access to the script. This is in marked contrast to the traditional Sherlock Holmes type investigator, who can look at a footprint and immediately ascertain *everything* about the suspect – how much change he had in his pocket, the mole on his butt, the size of his glass eye, [2] favorite turn-on, payroll deduction tendencies, political preference, and of course, his astro-

---

[1] Studies have shown hashish is easier to sell door-to-door.
[2] Actually, one size fits all, except in Texas.

logical sign.

Along similar lines, every possible question is answered at the end of a Sherlock type story. The guy was a know-it-all, which he further accented by having the brain dead Watson hang out with him. [3] But at the close of a film noir caper, zillions of questions remain. This reflects both the dark ambiguity of real life, and the fact that screenwriters drink too much. The classic convoluted example is *The Big Sleep*, from the Raymond Chandler novel of the same name. When director Howard Hawks called the writer about a little detail – like who committed one of the murders – Chandler said "You got me." Now Hawks might just have caught him at a bad time, like on a whiskey coma morning.

(Repeat after me: never call writers in the morning, or they might tell you to be fruitful and multiply but not in those exact words.) But in a later interview (which should be noted was *not* attempted in the morning), Chandler said story-ending answers were not important. We will now pause a moment while writing teachers everywhere gnash their teeth. For Chandler, as well as most film noir writers, the key was the journey through the tale. He wanted to write stories people would read even if the last page was missing. [4] If Sherlock Holmes' creator Sir Arthur Conan Doyle had not already been planted, this "to hell with the conclusion" philosophy would have done the trick. But of course you do not get to be called *"Sir"* by rocking the storytelling boat.

Film noir's undercutting of the American dream is made more palatable by a generous helping of dark humor. *Chinatown* is the ultimate example of this. The story revolves around the drowning of the Los Angeles water commissioner . . . during a drought. The heavy behind this move to control the city's water

---

[3] Viewer surveys reveal no one actually believed Watson was a doctor, except for his mother.

[4] This position also provides a boost to used book sales.

is *Noah* Cross, (John Huston), who also happens to be the commissioner's father-in-law. As a minor character observes early, this story has got "water on the brain." Even Nicholson's biting dialogue, as Jake Gittes, often has an aquatic angle, such as his favorite analogy for speed, "Quicker than the wind from a duck's ass."

The film is set in the late 1930s Los Angeles. Nicholson's character runs a detective agency specializing in the documentation of sexually wayward spouses. Since one of the basic tenets of noir film is that people are unreliable, the adultery business is booming and so is his agency. Indeed, this is the only variation from the genre's standard private eye – Nicholson has folding stuff in his pocket and the clothes look good. Bogie sometimes looked as though he'd slept in his trench coat, as if he were breaking it in for Columbo.

The water commissioner's alleged wife hires Nicholson to see if hubby has a skirt on the side. He appears to; the romantic scandal hits the papers and the next thing Jack knows the real wife (Faye Dunaway) has him by the proverbial short hairs.[5] But when the commissioner turns up dead, Nicholson and the widow team up, both in and out of the sheets. Dunaway is the standard man-eating nympho noir woman, right down to having sex with Daddy – incest being something the original films of the genre could only hint at.[6]

Early on it is revealed Nicholson used to be a police detective in Chinatown, and this becomes the fatalistic slant of the story. Most noir films have this German Expressionistic (boogie,

---

[5] The author naturally abhors this guttural slang but regrettably, the noir genre requires it.

[6] And they had to be very broad hints, since the period censorship office could find three meanings in a double-entendre.

boogie, boogie) angle where you cannot escape your destiny.[7] The hero might just as well stay in the sack, especially since the noir woman is generally there too. It wouldn't be like going to bed without your supper. As it is, at one point Nicholson has to tell Dunaway enough already; 37 times in one night is plenty, even if you're a dick.

Director Polanski spoofs the torrid sex associated with this bitch-kitty genre. (What do you think, was "bitch-kitty" too much?) At a time when Polanski could have given the viewer explicit bedroom action he opts not to (yeah, bummer). Thus, we only get to see the bedded Nicholson and Dunaway after all the vinyl sheet stuff is over, with the first film shot being his limp arm hanging off the bed with a lit cigarette. Besides the image's obvious "he's shot his wad" message, it also pays homage to a pivotal noir icon – the smoking cigarette. Back in the 1940's, when it was against movie censorship rules to even look hot, the cigarette was one overworked sex symbol. The burning stick in a person's mouth, all that lighting-up cigarette foreplay . . . must one draw you a dirty picture? No other movie symbol, with the possible exception of the good old train going into the tunnel, ever had so much sexual impact.

While *Chinatown* unfortunately doesn't give you all the sexual jump-start it could, it does provide the ever popular twisted violence – all in keeping with basic film noir guidelines. The most striking example is Polanski's mobster cameo, where the diminutive director is called a "midget" by Nicholson. Not a good move by our hero. Before you can say, "Watch your nose, Jack," Polanski whips out a switchblade as big as a horse's leg and makes like that

---

[7] We'll be returning periodically to fatalism updates about Nicholson's past in *Chinatown*. But for now you might want to brush-up on *The Cabinet of Dr. Caligari*. If this all seems rather ambiguous – welcome to film noir.

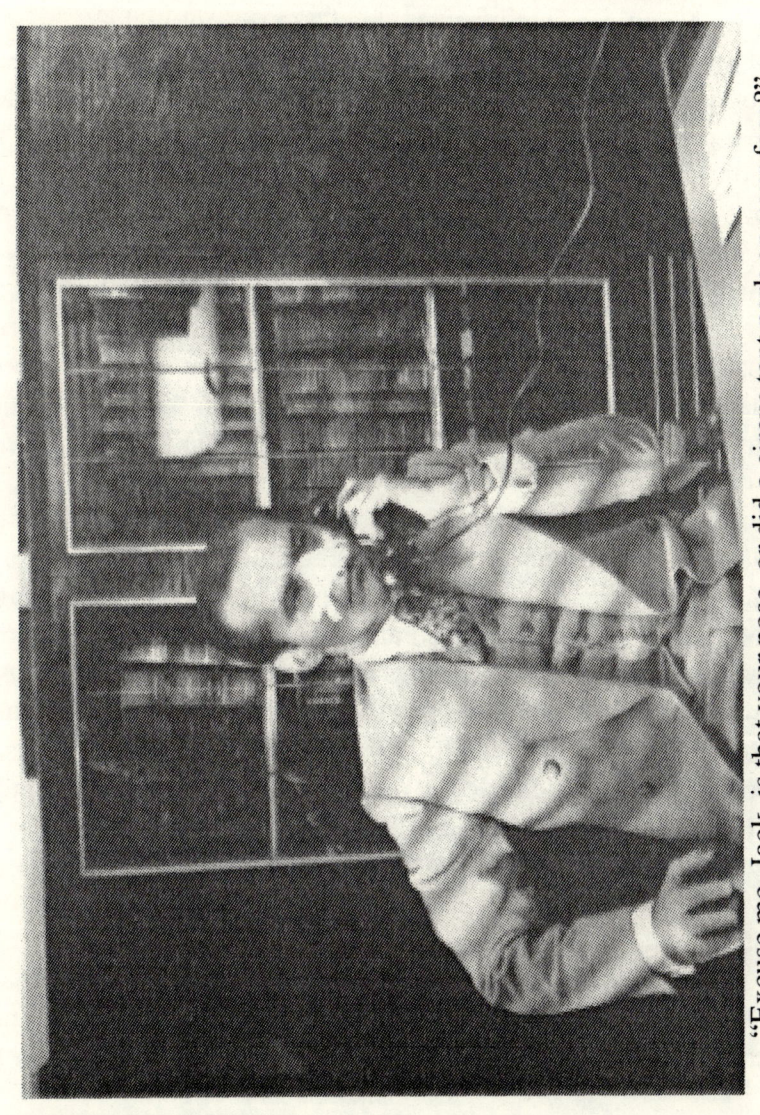

"Excuse me, Jack, is that your nose, or did a circus tent park on your face?" (Nicholson in *Chinatown*.)

schnoz is a Halloween pumpkin. Consistent with the film's dark comedy use of water references, Polanski's "midget" then threatens, "Next time I cut it off and feed it to my goldfish."[8]

Besides the shock of seeing your star nearly lose his proboscis (it just isn't done), there's the black humor of a nosy detective getting his beak snipped. Plus, it is an ongoing reason for more dark yucks; with Nicholson soon sporting a bandage the size of a water buffalo on his wounded snoot, references are constantly being made to it. And Jack, in the smart-ass tradition of so many past noir dicks, always has a great comeback, from "I cut myself shaving," to it "Only hurts when I breathe." However, the real topper is when an old nemesis taunts him with, "Someone slam a bedroom window on it?" He replies, "Your wife got a little too excited. She crossed her legs too quickly. You get what I mean?" Freud would have loved this genre.

Having Nicholson's schnozzola in stitches for much of the film also underlines noir's basic tenet, that it's a butt-ugly world. If you've noticed, most other genres tend to refrain from having their star's noses bayonetted and bandaged. Besides being distracting, think of the wind resistance problems it would have caused for Fred and Ginger. And this says nothing of wrecking a film's romantic mood by hard-to-smooch-around bandages. Plus, it could throw classic dialogue off. For instance, when Bogie says, "Here's looking at you, kid," in *Casablanca*, there would be no guarantee that he could even *see* Ingrid Bergman over a heavily wrapped snout, short of crossing his eyes, which invariably throws off a magic moment.

After the to-die-for sex scene between Nicholson and Dunaway that director Polanski tragically keeps from the audience (in a film democracy one should always give the public what

---

[8] Polanski excels at dark comedy, see especially his *Fearless Vampire Killers or: Pardon Me, But Your Teeth are in My Neck.*

it wants), more information is revealed about Nicholson's troubled Chinatown past. [9] He had tried to help a lover before and instead she had bought the farm. At this point, Dunaway should have raised her hand and said, "Excuse me but given noir's fatalistic bent, this doesn't seem to bode well for me." Okay, so maybe "bode" isn't the right word but the point remains, the girl should have known enough to be on the next Pacific Electric out of there.

As with all noir women, Dunaway does keep information from the hero, like that incest thing with Daddy. Yet, in this *Twilight Zone* of genres (Rod Serling would have made a great noir detective), she is less manipulative than the standard, you should excuse the noir expression, "bitch goddess." In fact, she can be downright sissified whenever Nicholson mentions her daddy the ogre. She stutters, loses her train of thought, lights dozens of cigarettes (even if she already has dozens going), and just generally acts as if she'd won the caffeine coffee drink-off.

Every time Nicholson visits her palatial dump, with the wall-to-wall servants, he hangs out in the backyard with a Japanese gardener. (Noir detectives get lonely, too.) Moreover, like all filthy rich noir women, Dunaway keeps him waiting 6-10 days. Anyhow, Hirohito the gardener is forever working round a little pond and mumbling what sounds like, "Bad for glass." [10] Nicholson tends to act rather condescending towards him, because after all, that's one of the perks of being a star. But eventually (remember the noir dick is no Sherlock Holmes), he realizes the gardener is saying "Bad for grass." The pond has salt water in it, and the

---

[9] In noir films to-die-for sex is more than just an expression. One need go no further than the titles of several classics in the genre – *Kiss of Death*, *Kiss the Blood Off My Hands*, *Murder, My Sweet* . . . Thus, whenever you get *hot*, be extra careful.

[10] The standard dialogue for noir's Asian characters has never exactly enhanced East-West relations.

drowned water commissioner had salt water in his lungs, as well as . . . we won't go into that right now. Plus, Nicholson finds a pair of glasses in the pond similar to those worn by the commissioner. [11] Dust off the blue ribbons; Jack's ready to go to the head of the tough guy detective class.

So close but he screws up. He figures the murderer must be Dunaway. And blaming the noir woman is not a bad assumption. After all, it worked for Bogie in *The Maltese Falcon* and Fred MacMurray in *Double Indemnity*. [12] But Dunaway is innocent and Nicholson has to do some fast thinking, because like a putz, he has told the police where to pick her up. It's not like he normally rats or anything, but the fuzz were getting ready to include him in the murder rap. And it's so hard to stay film noir cool if you're in the big house with a cell mate named Bubba. Besides, Bogie sent Mary Astor up river at the close of *The Maltese Falcon*, so it's not like Nicholson broke some noir code.

As he gets Dunaway off to what he thinks is safety (note the author's subtle suggestion of noir's evil fate) it dawns on her the glasses couldn't have belonged to her drowned husband; they are bifocals and her former main squeeze wasn't that blind. Nicholson is less than pleased. Noir dicks get enough overtime as it is. Especially when they think they're all done and could go home and listen to *Crime Busters* on the radio.

Now listen up. Since bifocals are usually associated with geezers, Nicholson takes a wild guess and zeros in on the only Methuselah in the script (Huston's Noah Cross) as the probable murderer. Good guess but Jack plays it all wrong. He tells the

---

[11] One lens of the glasses is shattered, a standard situation in film noir, symbolizing both the fragileness of life and an easy way to economize on used props.

[12] Unfortunately, because of Nick at Night's *My Three Sons*, it is now impossible to watch *Double Indemnity* without giggling.

guy what he knows, like Huston is going to reward him with the "Sam Spade Dick of the Year" award.

So quicker than you can say, "Dummy up, Jack," he finds a 45-caliber pistol stuck in his ear. This is never a good development, even if you have a wax build-up. He's forced to tell Huston (surprise, surprise) the whereabouts of daughter Dunaway and his daughter/granddaughter. Given his past track record with the young Dunaway, this is not the most promising of developments, unless maybe your ancestors immigrated here from Sodom and Gomorrah. But one interesting development in the Nicholson-Huston meeting is the comment the latter makes about incest, murder, and all-around corruption, three of Huston's favorite pastimes: "Most people don't have to face the fact that at the right time they're capable of anything."

This is chilling stuff, like that Raymond Chandler title, *The Baby in the Icebox*. The dark side of the American dream doesn't get any darker. Well it does, but the records of the relationship between President Gerald Ford and Pee Wee Herman won't be de-classified for years. Until then (watch your local listings), *Chinatown* has sickly gone where no previous noir film had ventured.

Polanski had made it his in-your-face mission to accent all the noir negatives, as if he'd taken graduate classes in pulling people's chains. But it is a logical development for someone with his background. As a Jewish youth in World War II Poland, he had played hide and seek with the Nazis for the duration of the conflict. Polanski was captured at one point, and German soldiers had used him for an impromptu game of target practice. Hardly a recommended exercise but great experience for a noir director, or a cruise director. Then later, as he was establishing his international film career, that merry band called the Manson family did in his wife and several close friends.

Is it any wonder the guy relates to film noir and has a cameo where he nearly gives Nicholson the ultimate nose job?

Noir is like Polanski's own story, though maybe not quite so macabre, because it doesn't get much worse than target practicing
Nazis and family get-togethers with the Mansons. Even now the
ongoing bizarre private life of Polanski continues, since he is still
wanted in this country for jumping bail on charges of jumping a
minor – standard plot action for three out of four noir films. [13]
Before fleeing to Paris, where he still lives, Polanski enjoyed adding the following postscript to his signature, when asked for his
autograph: "I'd like to tell you a bit more about myself but I can't
because of the trial."

As we now break for an introspective sidebar, which comes
your way at no extra charge, a building block of my youth is about
to be called into question. I was always taught to accept yourself
for who you are – but what if you're Charles Manson, or the
current serial killer of the month? (Excuse me while I call my
mom on this and I'll get back to you.) Returning to the 45 in
Jack's ear, the Dunaway hiding spot he is forced to reveal is naturally in L.A.'s Chinatown. Otherwise, people are going to start
asking questions about the film's title. There is a confrontation
between Dunaway and Huston. She shoots a hole in his shoulder
(a popular moment with most audiences), and then seems to escape by car with her daughter/sister. But that ugly old noir fate
kicks in and the police start blasting away at the departing car.

Suddenly comes the nonstop blare of Dunaway's car horn
as her now distant automobile rolls to a stop. But this slowdown
takes a while, since she is driving one of those big ass block-long
'30s Packards. Unfortunately, you know immediately what has
happened, unless you're one of those people who always go for
popcorn at pivotal plot moments. (And be more careful where

---

[13] At the time this happened it was rumored his next film would be
Close Encounters With the Third Grade. This was never con-
firmed but several associates from this period remember him forever whistling "Thank Heaven for Little Girls."

you put your goddamn feet on the way out, too!) Anyway, earlier in the film she'd been having a conversation with Nicholson in the car, during which time she tearfully leaned forward (as manipulative noir women are want to do when they're on a roll), inadvertently causing the car horn to suddenly blare in an otherwise quiet moment – scaring many viewers out of a full year's growth, with numerous older patrons simply jumping straight to heaven. (Actually, being a noir audience, they probably went to hell). Regardless, for surviving viewers, it seems obvious Dunaway was shot and had fallen forward over the horn.

Naturally, one is hoping it is not a serious wound but since this is a noir film, you're not placing any major bets on Dunaway popping up and doing the hokey pokey. This was a wise decision on your part, because when you get an opportunity to see her up close you can't help thinking she'd been in a motorcade in downtown Dallas.

Dunaway's daughter/sister freaks, as often happens when someone you're close to has her head explode all over your new outfit. And who is there to comfort her and take the girl away – the evil incestuous father/grandfather Noah Cross. The perfect noir (rhymes with gore) ending, though Polanski had to fight hard for it, since the original scripted conclusion had Dunaway getting away with the girl. Geez, with a beautiful day in the neighborhood ending like that, they might just as well have had Mr. Rogers play Noah Cross.

And what about Nicholson's Jake? Well, he's reduced to a state not unlike being smacked with a two-by-four. All he's capable of doing is one ongoing vowel movement, with the only decipherable words being "as little as possible" – a flashback to what they used to say he could do when he was a cop in Chinatown. Meaning, hello fatalism. Once again he has tried to help a lover and instead has gotten her killed, something you should never put on your computer dating card.

A fellow dick from his agency tries to comfort him with,

"Forget it Jake, it's Chinatown." But you can't help thinking Nicholson's character is going to be sitting in the window with a drool cup for years to come. As it is, co-workers are leading him away like it's time to go to the film noir nursing home, a black and white dump with lots of Venetian blinds, bad lighting, long-legged nurses in slit dresses and high heels who specialize in pushing wheelchair types down staircases, and where the only visitors are pop-eyed psychotic types who look like Peter Lorre. And like every other film noir day, a dirty gray sky covered Chinatown like a sneeze shield from the land of the giants.

In contrast, licking his lips, Huston not only takes the girl off at the close (noir's a genre that can keep that sinking feeling going well into next week), he also gets away with both drowning his water commissioner son-in-law and making millions on illegal land dealing related to the murder. Ah, the good life.

This is not a feel-good sort of film, unless maybe you're Guido the hit man. The only golden rule for noir movies represents disposable income. This genre teaches that all things bad not only triumph, they get to have fun at it, too. Drawing from another noir film, the secret to the dark side is "Do it first, do it yourself, and keep on doing it" (this covers illicit sex, robbery, murder, and the heinous crime of your choice). Not only will this philosophy make you the big noir winner in the crap shoot of life, eventually you'll even bludgeon yourself into an honored status. As Huston's character says, "Politicians, ugly buildings, and whores all get respectable if they last long enough." He might have added this also applies to those who enjoy raping relatives, the environment, and the next thing on the auction block. Yes, consistent with *Chinatown*'s water motif, one might say a really good noir film makes the viewer want to go somewhere and wash up.

I would add more but what with my paper route and church choir rehearsals, and volunteer work at the orphanage, I sometimes miss things. Anyway, I'm told there are many people who admire film noir, though you don't see them walking around in the daytime.

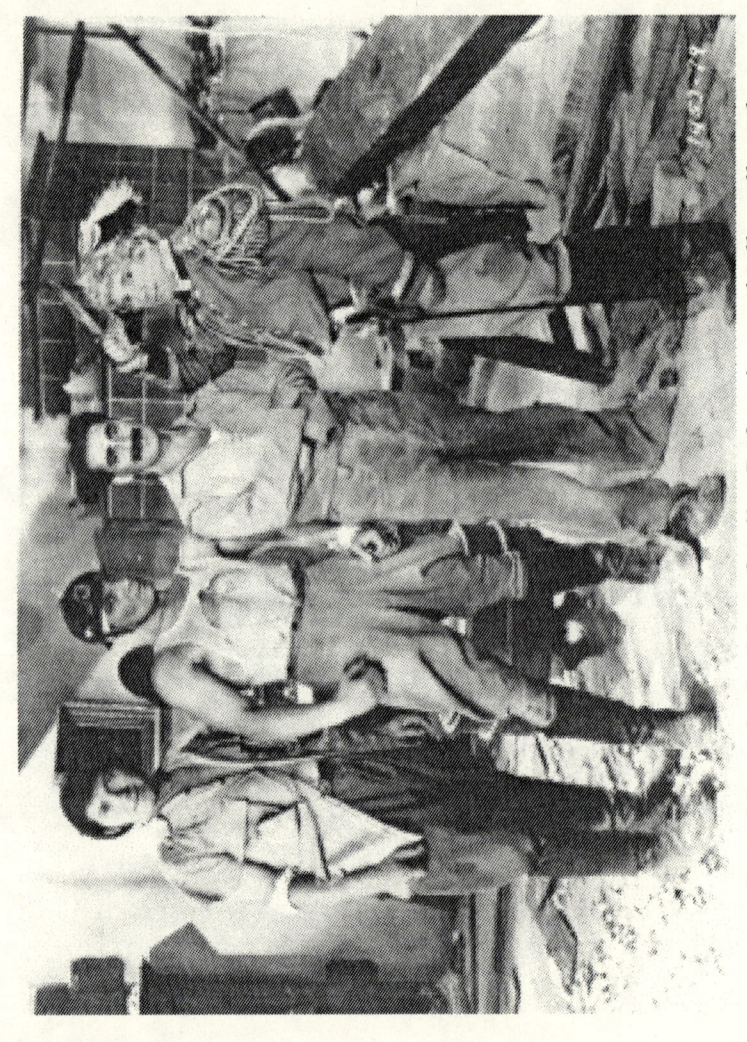

Insanity ran in the Marx family. In fact, it practically galloped.
(Left to right -- Chico, Zeppo, Groucho, and Harpo in *Duck Soup*.)

DUCK SOUP

"Married! I can see you right now in the kitchen,
bending over a hot stove, but I can't see the stove."
—Groucho to Margaret Dumont in
Duck Soup

Yes, Harpo could speak in real life. Now that we have that perennial question out of the way things should move along much more quickly. In the 1930s Groucho and his brothers went forth . . . or fifth, if you count Gummo. Who, you say? Ok, maybe a family score card would be helpful. The brothers, in order by age and with given names in parentheses, were: Chico (real name Leonard), Harpo (Adolph), Groucho (Julius), Gummo (Milton), and Zeppo (Herbert). You can see why they'd want to change their names.

Chico's nickname was derived from his lifelong chasing of women (chicks), a pastime from which he was never distracted, even on his honeymoon. Thus, Chico should be pronounced with the short i rather than as "cheek-o".[1] Because people have been saying it incorrectly since 1914 B.C. (before Chaplin), this bit of info invariably impresses the folks around the punch bowl. There'll be loads of "hmmms" washing over you, so bring a towel. Harpo's alias is a bit more obvious, unless you've recently had a lobotomy. It came from playing the harp (also known as a piano in the nude).[2]

----

[1] There's an old Chico anecdote about one of his soon to be sexual conquests telling him a "real woman" could keep him home. His alleged reply, "It would have to be a big woman."

[2] Interestingly enough, at home Harpo enjoyed playing in the nude. In fact, several prominent visitors to his home had the rather startling experience of being ushered into his musical presence while he played el buffo. Our Harpo always acted like it was the most natural of things, which, if you were a Marx Brother, it might have been.

Groucho's nickname came from a grouchy personality, on screen and off. Like Tommy Smothers, Groucho's mom really didn't like him best, either. Gummo's handle came from wearing gum-soled shoes. Fittingly, for someone with a non-personality, you didn't hear Gummo either. God only knows where Zeppo got his alias. Everyone had a different story. Groucho credited it to the World War I flying Zeppelins. (And they say Groucho never drank more than one glass of wine at a setting?) Harpo claimed it was a variation of a now thankfully forgotten vaudeville act called Mr. Zippo. But remember, this is from a man who liked to play naked as a jaybird. Chico and Gummo's explanation seems the most logical (and boring); it was drawn from the rural nickname of Zeb, when the Marx clan briefly owned an Illinois farm. Your vote on the Zeppo question will be taken shortly, so remember to review your options.

As a scandalous sidenote (something all the popular literature has), the Marx farm was a World War I attempt at a draft dodge for the brothers. It's always suspicious when a longtime New York Jewish theatrical family turns up on an Illinois farm. The boys did, however, have rural pride. When expecting urban company they bought large eggs and planted them in their hens' nests. The draft board, evidently not fans of eggs or comedy (it's those uniforms), nixed this dodge idea and demanded of Marx mother/agent Minnie at least one of her boys "over there." But unlike the tough decision of, say, *Sophie's Choice*, Minnie just went with the least talented – Gummo. Actually it had almost been a dead heat with Zeppo but he was underage.

All five brothers were at some time part of the team, although never simultaneously. Gummo did not rejoin the team after the war. [3] Zeppo replaced him, only to leave early in the

---

[3] Gummo had never really been comfortable on stage, which would also be true of Zeppo. Even the teenage Harpo, during his first public performance, wet his pants. Gee, is there a hint of a stage mother here?

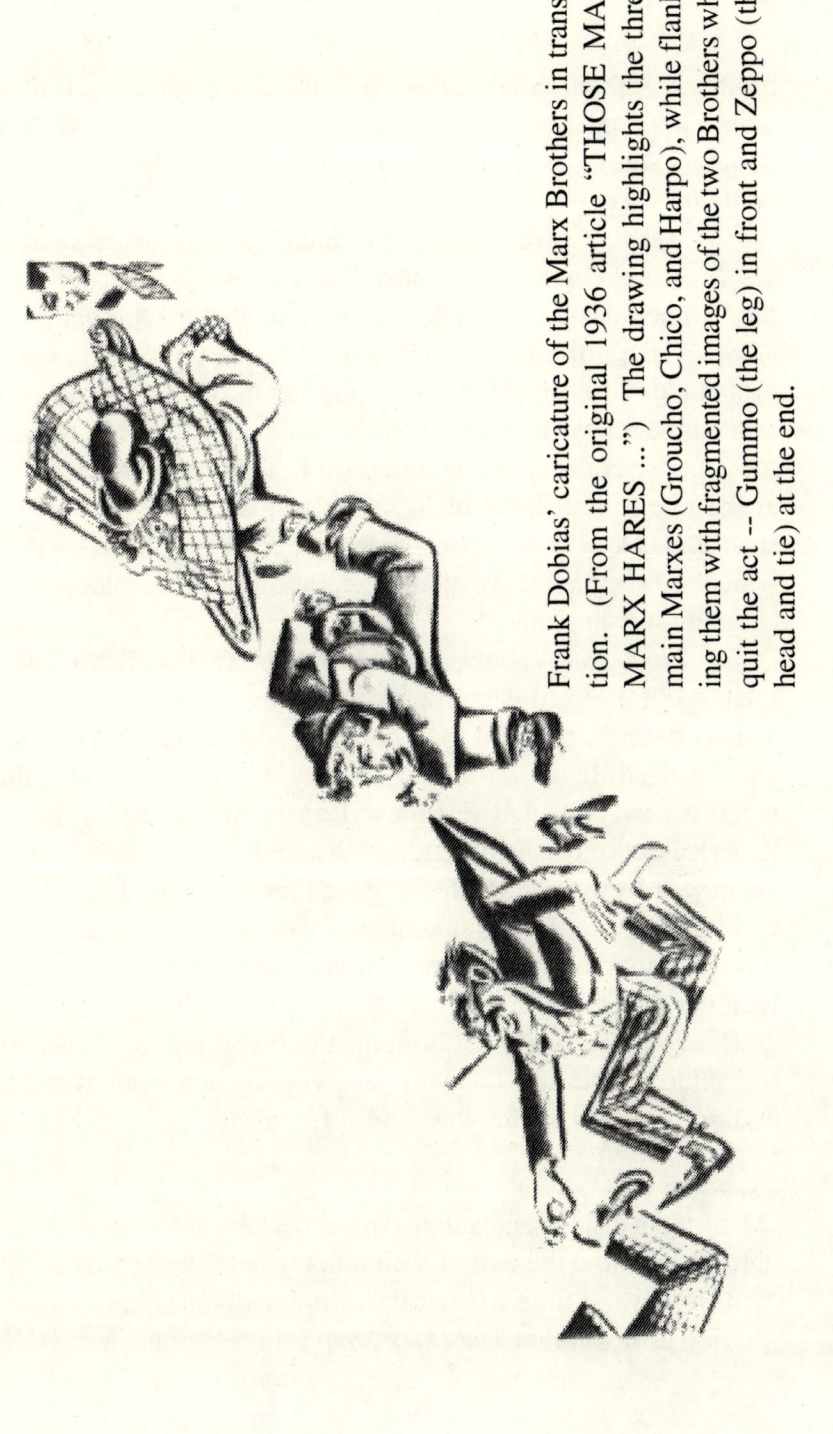

Frank Dobias' caricature of the Marx Brothers in transition. (From the original 1936 article "THOSE MAD MARX HARES ...") The drawing highlights the three main Marxes (Groucho, Chico, and Harpo), while flanking them with fragmented images of the two Brothers who quit the act -- Gummo (the leg) in front and Zeppo (the head and tie) at the end.

brother's screen career, after the critics threatened to find out where he lived. For fans of the team, the title of a later Marx Brothers study said it about right – *Groucho, Harpo, Chico and Sometimes Zeppo.*

Yet there was another "brother," sort of. Frequent co-star Margaret Dumont was called "the fifth Marx Brother," while the "Sometimes Zeppo" was still with the team. Dumont generally played a stuffy mountain of a dowager (to get all of her in the viewfinder you needed an aerial photograph), who was the constant high society target of the brothers and off whom they bounced roughhouse comedy and assorted fruit. Dumont's character was at the intellectual level of moss. Thus, Groucho's put-downs, such as his *Duck Soup* crack, "I'm prepared to fight for your honor, which is more than you ever did" seemed almost harmless as they zoomed over her head. [4]

Duck Soup is now considered their greatest film but when released in 1933, this stun gun satire went right in the toilet. [5] This is because the film took potshots at government (Groucho was crooked dictator Rufus T. Firefly of Freedonia) at a time when a newly elected President Roosevelt was trying to pull America out of the Depression. [6] While Roosevelt offered the country a New Deal, Rufus T. gave Freedonia an old deal . . . a regular false shuffle. Remember, if you're not cynical, you're probably not paying attention. (If you have to trust everyone, at least cut the cards.)

Duck Soup did not limit itself, however, to alienating period audiences in just one way. As with its men from Marx, everything about the film was a bit different for the '30s. For in-

---

[4] Many team insiders, including Groucho, claimed Dumont's screen obtuseness (note the author's diplomacy here) was no act.

[5] And this was a time when toilets were really nasty.

[6] Period critics called *The Duck Soup* Marxes "comedemons."

stance, this was a time when *all* comedies were supposed to have a sappy love story subplot. (It's in the Hollywood bylaws, page 62, just after the restrictions on dating Munchkins.) The theory was people couldn't handle 100 percent comedy in a film without going a little crazy – like when you break into someone's house and iron their clothes. And since most comedians were too goofy-looking to double as a legitimate love interest, that meant saddling the plot with some dimpled-cheeked sweeties making kissy faces every six minutes. A worse case scenario had these two singing their gooey devotions to each other . . . a regular diabetic alert.

The ultimate gone-to-hell situation, however, was operetta duets, also known as high class screaming, or music set to melodrama. The key reason the Marxes' often celebrated *A Night at the Opera* has lost brownie points with today's audiences is those straight operetta numbers. Moreover, there's a sense of hypocrisy (comedy isn't always pretty), since the Marxes' only allegiance normally is to nose-thumbing anarchy. For most of the film they deflate the pomposity of high art (opera), yet they periodically let the young lovers exercise their lungs without ever bashing them.

One longs, instead, for the irreverent consistency of *Duck Soup*'s close where, despite the victory of their side (Freedonia), the Marxes cannot keep from bombarding Margaret Dumont with fruit when she does her operatic rendition of their national anthem. (This scene would later inspire a zany businessman to market a pocket *club* to be used on noisy audience members – "It says shut-up in every language!") Regardless, there was no love story subplot in *Duck Soup*. Outlandish as this seems to today's audience, this lack of romance contributed to a loss of 1930s box office, when movies represented more of a variety show for the masses.

Duck Soup even broke a Marx Brothers' rule. Normally, Harpo did a solo on his you-know-what, while Chico had a number on the piano (more of that variety show flavor). But as beautiful as Harpo's music is, if you're into that harp crap, it has a highbrow flavor which invariably derails whatever semblance of a plot has surfaced, especially if it puts you to sleep. In contrast, Chico's piano (which is sort of a horizontal harp with hammers) is not quite so disruptive, given that it is always played for humorous effect. Still, like them or not, these musical solos take away from the progression of the film. [7]

One might paraphrase a Woody Allen story here – a movie is like a shark. It must constantly move forward, or it dies. And in the case of the Harpo/Chico solos, what we have are several dead film segments. Groucho himself said it best in *Horse Feathers* when, just prior to a brother's number, he walked to the camera and in direct address to the viewer observed, "I've got to stay here, but there's no reason why you folks shouldn't go out into the lobby until this thing blows over."

While *Duck Soup*'s lack of these musical interludes is a big hit with today's audience, 1930s viewers were steamed about the omissions. Why, there were even letters to the *New York Times* about it . . . but the Union survived, and so did the Marxes. Though as in all creative endeavors not adequately appreciated by the public, the artists (that would be the Marxes) were, how shall we say, *pissed*. But that's another story.

Duck Soup begins with Groucho being late to his own inauguration, which you can do when you've already been made dictator for life . . . with parking privileges, too. Being part of an equal opportunity family, Chico and Harpo are spies for Freedonia's arch rival, Sylvania (which like that 1950s television set of the

---

[7] Groucho was the perfect musician; he could play several instruments . . . but he seldom did.

same name, sounded impressive but didn't work very well).[8] Chico and Harpo's cover is a peanut stand in front of Groucho's palace. The pushcart business isn't much but it provides a little income while they learn how to tail people (Philip Marlowe and Sam Spade need not worry).

Of course, in their apprentice spy favor, Chico and Harpo do enjoy the trade. For instance, when they are asked by their Sylvanian contact what day they shadowed Groucho, Chico replies, "We shadow him all day . . . Shadowday [Saturday]. Some joke, huh, boss?" Sure it's rank but he so enjoys telling stinko puns you cannot help thinking kindly of him as you fantasize about braining him before he utters another one.

The peanut stand is also the "catalyst" (this is what is known as a Ph.D. dissertation word) for a vendor war with Edgar "Slow Burn" Kennedy, who runs an aggressive lemonade business on the same block. Kennedy was a character actor best known for his appearances in Laurel and Hardy comedies. His "Slow Burn" nickname came from Stan and Ollie innocently yet methodically annoying him into a killer rage just this side of *Jack the Ripper*.[9] Anyway, the lemonade-peanut conflict begins with Chico and Harpo tormenting (what they did best) Kennedy by making a

_____

[8] In his standard Rodney "no respect" Dangerfield part, Zeppo plays Groucho's secretary, with the high point – and the term is used loosely – being when Harpo cuts his hat in half. After *Duck Soup*, Zeppo did a "take this job and shove it" number, retiring from acting. Ironically, within the Marx family, he was considered the funniest brother. Go figure.

[9] *Duck Soup*'s director, Leo McCarey, knew Kennedy from the days when McCarey had molded and teamed Laurel and Hardy. Yes, Hal Roach normally receives credit for these things. But that's merely because he who lives longest – and Roach nearly beat Methuselah's record – gets to write the history.

106

game of taking his hat. [10] Harpo the firebug later ups the ante by burning it. Kennedy responds by tipping over the peanut cart. Harpo, of course, gets the *last word* . . . actually, that's not a good description for Harpo. Let's just say he wins by taking off his shoes and washing his feet in Kennedy's large lemonade container. It's amazing how quickly a little trick like that causes business to drop off.

The humor in the lemonade-peanut war is based in what comedy scholarship calls the "tit-for-tat" routine. Yeah, yeah, it sounds a little suggestive but cut the academics some slack, it gets pretty boring in those ivory towers, not to mention the difficulty of having pizza delivered. Scholars have to spice things up somehow, or no one would read their articles. It's a sad life, and so little money for partying. Tit-for-tat simply means a polite and orderly approach to comic violence (always popular in America) as the participants take turns with their destruction. [11]

One might also call the tit-for-tat routine organized chaos, because the combatants often methodically put the kibosh on everything this side of the international dateline. Yet at all times there is the comic incongruity of patiently letting someone level something of yours before you flatten something of theirs. One must not lose that thin veneer of civilization when doing someone dirty. And as the central satirical focus of *Duck Soup* suggests, similar misunderstandings can lead to real (evening news type) wars, where there are no retakes, and the action never stops, except for the occasional laxative commercial.

----

[10] One half expects punster Chico to also unload some "lemonade" crack at Kennedy, but thankfully he spares us.

[11] There are, of course, other non-academic definitions for "tit-for-tat" but in the interest of potential book sales to minors, we won't go into that here. But pictures can be obtained if you send $29.95 and a self-addressed stamped envelope to "The Rest of the Story," Ball U.

It is fitting that the lemonade-peanut aggression scenes should have little dialogue, because *Duck Soup* director Leo McCarey's motto was, "Set 'em up." [12] Whoops, wrong tagline. No, his filming maxim was, "Do it visually." He never really knew what to make of Groucho (no one really did, except the mustached one's ex-wives). [13] Naturally, McCarey gravitated towards Harpo the mime, whose magic trench coat pockets could produce any sight gag this side of a comic apocalypse, as well as an occasional cup of steaming hot coffee. Thus, the most celebrated routine of *Duck Soup* is the silent mirror scene, where Harpo (trying to steal Freedonia's war plans) outsmarts Groucho by passing as his reflection in a tour de silly performance. It's that rare occasion when machine-gun mouth Groucho says nary a word. [14]

As a side note on the physical appearances of the three main Marx Brothers (apologies to Gummo and Zeppo . . . not), Groucho, Harpo, and Chico could easily pass for each other starting with early childhood pranks. The most provocative examples came in adulthood, however, when Chico (remember the origins of that nickname) used to commit adultery in Harpo's name.

The inspired mirror sequence, where Groucho seems to be more than the sum of his reflection, also works on several additional levels – always a promising development when you want to impress potential lovers, or suck-up to your dissertation com-

---

[12] McCarey, like the stereotypical Irishman, enjoyed a good drink. Moreover, as a close friend of W. C. Fields (charter member of the drinking hall of fame), McCarey spent many an evening bending his elbow. It has even been suggested he ghosted the W. C. line, "It's hard to tell where Hollywood ends and DT's begin."

[13] After divorcing his third wife Groucho still occasionally dated her. When asked why, he replied, "I like to be near my money."

[14] Do you think the use of the word "nary" in this sentence adds a certain poetic touch to the passage? You're not just saying that to be nice? Thank you very much.

mittee. [15] First, despite Groucho's advanced con artist skills, he invariably falls victim to his brothers. It's rather like a comedy version of "You can't go home again." The most studied Groucho derailments come at the hands of Harpo, [16] in part because these are traditionally the two most popular brothers and they are the most radically different. Having Harpo forever best Groucho is similar to a mute shouting down a motor mouth. Harpo is a force of nature – a natural disaster with attitude.

A second way in which the mirror sequence works as a Marx Brothers metaphor (if you're keeping track of this stuff, which will be on the quiz), is that things are seldom what they seem to be . . . especially in Korean restaurants. This covers everything from Harpo sorcery, to Groucho and Chico manipulating and murdering what is supposed to be the English language. For instance, when Groucho first meets Margaret Dumont in *Duck Soup* he tells her, "If you can't get a taxi you can leave in a huff." Ok, so this verbal slapstick is not exactly Oscar material, but Groucho puts it across with pure chutzpa (pronounce the *ch* with a strong *yeching*, as if spitting up a hairball). The Marxes constantly encourage the viewer to look at things from a different perspective, not unlike the life lessons Robin Williams gives his students years later in *Dead Poets Society*, such as looking at the world from the top of his desk. [17]

A final example of how the mirror sequence "reflects" other

---

[15] The cynical, world-weary type might suggest the ideal development would be a sexual partner on your dissertation committee, which would, of course, give a whole new meaning to the oral exam.

[16] Actually, Harpo used all his limbs.

[17] Groucho and Williams have a lot in common. Besides both being mammals, their humor has a stream-of-conscience intensity which is hilarious, though it often frightens small animals.

Marx Brothers material is its surrealism – the arrested development factor. This movement, which originated in France just in
time for the Marxes, attempted to express in art the workings of
the unconscious. Thus, artists could start charging for their nap
time, too. In America polite critics called it "Dream Art," but the
general public merely thought of it as a bad day with Alice through
the looking glass, or bedlam rearranged by James Thurber. [18] But
the relationship between one pioneering surrealist, Salvador of
the melting clocks Dali, and the Marxes bears noting.

This zany showman, the public's idea of a crazy genius
(with that dippity-do mustache), went bonkers over the Marxes,
especially Harpo, whom Dali saw as the ultimate wizard of odd.
The artist called Harpo the most surreal of actors, a title possibly
assisted by the fact Dali was one of those guests first introduced
to Harpo while the comedian practiced his music in the nude.
Dali would do several paintings of Harpo (with clothes), and the
comedian reciprocated by teaching him how to shoot toy arrows
from a harp string. (Is that getting into the spirit of surrealism or
what?) [19]

Naturally, Dali (there's really nothing natural about the
man) especially liked *Duck Soup* because it is the best film showcase of Harpo's work. And if one were to generally apply a surrealist axiom to Marx material, given time to screw around like
that, it would be: attempting to make sense of this absurd world
is an open invitation to ridicule . . . and it could cause your brain

---

[18] Non-polite critics made comments about the surrealists' moth-
ers.

[19] Harpo had surrealist tendencies from the beginning. As a child
the already gambling Chico used to pawn everything that wasn't
bolted down in the Marx household. Little brother Harpo, to
safeguard his prize pocket watch, broke off its arms. Short of
melting it, Harpo couldn't have done a more Dali-like stunt.

to overheat. (Just remember, everyone is a little neurotic but sometimes nets might be in order.)

Despite the early spying activities of Chico and Harpo, Groucho eventually wins them over to Freedonia's side . . . an addition of questionable assistance. But the main thrust of the story (almost sounds erotic) remains the ongoing threat of war between Freedonia and Sylvania. What finally pushes them into conflict is Groucho's comic paranoia about the intentions of the enemy. In terms of film history (just a little erudition, please), Groucho's comic interpretation of a persecution complex has direct ties with the later darker paranoia of General Jack Ripper in *Dr. Strangelove or: How I Learned to Stop Worrying and Love the Bomb*.

Ripper starts an apocalyptic atomic war because he believes the fluoridation of America's water supply to be an evil plot hatched by the Commies (remember them?). For decades, of course, this country's foreign policy has been strongly anchored in good old-fashioned paranoia and other forms of hiding under the bed. So *Duck Soup* continues to be praised as a devastating satire of how megalomaniac leaders (read Rufus T. Firefly) can make the government of your choice jump the tracks. (Oh, it wasn't the end of the world . . . the decline, maybe.)

Duck Soup also manages to take pot shots at how gullible the public is. It was a timely lesson, too, given the then contemporary popularity in Germany and Italy of that Chuck Chaplin look-alike (Hitler) and the wannabe Caesar with the protruding lip (Mussolini).[20] Throughout *Duck Soup* Groucho manipulates everyone, save his brothers. By the time of the film's war *celebration*, the mustached one has even managed to suck his sib-

---

[20] When *Duck Soup* was released, Mussolini (Benny to his poker buddies) banned the film in Italy.

lings into the misguided patriotism of approaching battle. [21]

Whereas, most of *Duck Soup* had leisurely meandered around Groucho, who had leisurely meandered around the wealthy dumb as a post Margaret Dumont, the movie's lengthy battlefront conclusion does a devastating number on that less than glorious habit called war. Groucho helps this ever topical message along by varying his military uniform every two minutes, from Prussian formal with the spiked helmet suitable for weenie roasting, to the basic Davy Crockett casual look topped off with the simple wash and wear coonskin cap. [22] Ah yes, dressed to be killed . . . through the ages.

Groucho's *saturation* comedy ability to flood the airways with comedy is complimented during this drawn-out finale by Director McCarey's montage (French for "editing" and in café use – "cut my spaghetti please") of film clips. [23] Groucho has just sent out a call for help and McCarey cuts to footage of alleged assistance which includes everything from packs of baboons and schools of porpoises, to motorcycle cops and fire engines. It's *Bennie Hill* and *Laugh-In*, thirty-five years early.

The ultimate victory of Freedonia (the Marxes capture Sylvania's leader and celebrate by throwing fruit at his kisser) is a comment on both the triviality of war, and how it is frequently played out as some sort of super-macho game – especially when

---

[21] Woody Allen includes this "Marxist" musical comedy salute to war in his film *Hannah and Her Sisters*. What, you no longer like Allen? Well, don't kill the messenger here. And there's no truth to the rumor Allen will eventually make the movies *Hannah and Her Daughters* and *Honey, I F___ the Kids*.

[22] Always a fashion statement, though among naturalists it's more of a fashion risk.

[23] Groucho developed the verbal machine-gun approach as comedy self-defense – if the audience didn't like one joke he could be on to another before they ripped his lungs out.

Groucho had to pay a month's rent on the battlefield and buy ready made fox holes. Yes, war is like scuba diving, where your main goal of the day is to not die. In the final analysis (promises, promises), *Duck Soup* is a classic for insights like these, as well as providing a showcase for Marxian gall. [24] Like comic gangsters Baby Face Harpo and company, we celebrate the Marxes because they do the things we only dream about.

---

[24] This is a team who could knock off their parents and then beg the court for mercy since they were orphans.

CITIZEN KANE

The greatest movie of all time had the most
modest of film preview trailers – *Citizen Kane*,
"it's a coming attraction. At least, it's coming to
this theater, and we hope it's an attraction."

Yeah, this is the *Rosebud* movie, the worst kept secret this side of
Guess Who's Coming to Dinner?. Like an Alfred Hitchcock
cameo, it's hard for people to address the film without first discussing *Rosebud* – the last word uttered by the title character . . .
and the word which opens the film. For the next 119 minutes (if
you're counting) a reporter attempts to discover just what the
term meant to Orson Welles' great and terrible Kane. Like a film
noir detective, the reporter is ultimately screwed – he doesn't find
the answer. But the viewer, because he/she has stuck it out for
two hours of art house movie symbolism and other butt-busting
intellectual mind games, is rewarded with the fleeting sight of the
man's boyhood sled (*Rosebud*) being tossed into a fire of what
are supposed to be Kane's torchable possessions.

Yes, *Rosebud* represents the lost happiness and simplicity
of childhood and also underlines that old adage "you can't take it
with you," especially if you have a big sled. But don't worry,
sleds will be out of season for most people in the next life . . .
dress lightly. It's rather a smaltzy gooey close to an otherwise
harsh look at the American success story. It couldn't have been
more sentimental unless you'd made *Rosebud* be a puppy, which
would have thrown a whole new slant on the fire scene. [1]

---

[1] As a little nit-picking aside, when Kane whispers *Rosebud* and
cashes in, no one is within seven counties. Just who was supposed to have heard this? Did George Bailey have another second class angel hovering about? Some people do notice these
things. So there.

Late in Welles' own life, however, he revealed what would have been a very provocative story slant on just what *Rosebud* really meant. It seems that flamboyant newspaper magnate William Randolph Hearst, upon whose life *Citizen Kane* is based, had a very non-sled like use of the term *Rosebud*. It was, according to Welles' authorized biography, Hearst's nickname for the genitalia of his movie star mistress Marion Davies. Now *that* would have been a hot close to the movie. No wonder Hearst had a raging conniption about the film. Yes, it does tend to make men a little pissy when their pet name for a sweetie's . . . you know, becomes the key plot point in a major motion picture. At the same time it is tricky to complain about, unless you're into calling press conferences about *the* clitoris in you life. [2]

Instead, Hearst privately attempted to block the movie's release and have the master copy diced into banjo picks. [3] But some historians have suggested it was really Davies who was bent out of shape, just because a two hour search for the meaning of *Rosebud* rubbered her the wrong way . . . so to speak. Realistically, this explanation makes more sense, in that Hearst should have appreciated the fact that more men would identify with a character whose check-out line encompassed what they are always thinking about anyway, instead of a kid's sled, which would only speak to a tiny wuss factor. (There are on record only three card-carrying sentimentalists who have ever lasted until the *Rosebud* scene.)

As a side note, Steven Spielberg later paid $60,000 for the stand-in *Rosebud*, which did not go up the chimney. Obviously, many people could have given him a better deal on a used

---

[2] Upon reconsideration, the real meaning of *Rosebud* probably did have a sled-like meaning for Hearst, metaphorically – as in life's ultimate fun ride. If this helps any.

[3] Yes, he was mad enough to scare the dickens out of some little Keebler elves.

sled, plus thrown in some mittens and a muffler. But he said it was worth it, since *Rosebud* symbolizes film excellence. Of course, while most everyone enjoys symbols, the majority of people try to keep them under $60,000. Spielberg has since hung *Rosebud* on his library wall to inspire him to write scripts of *Citizen Kane* quality. [4] Remember when a pep talk was all a person needed, and sleds seldom cost as much as a house?

So how did this expensive sled story get made? Well, in the late 1930s Orson Welles' *War of the Worlds* radio broadcast so freaked out depression America that the nation really thought a Martian invasion was underway. His notoriety from this men from Mars scam (numerous weak hearts bought the farm out of fright, not to mention a truckload of babies who came early) put Welles in the national spotlight. While the program upset the nerve medicine set, most people, especially in the entertainment industry, were impressed with this young man's moxie.

Ok, imagine time passing. No, not that much, just a year or so. Welles has been invited to Hollywood by RKO, a studio so poor its personnel office used rented chapstick. The hope was this boy genius (Welles was all of 25), yet a movie novice, can save the studio's butt, or at least make the descent into the toilet interesting. It was a gamble but unlike most industries (outside of Las Vegas and Atlantic City), Hollywood was built on gambles. Take, for instance, the unlikely success story of a gorilla with gland problems becoming *King Kong*, or the hooker who finds happiness with a corporate prince in *Pretty Woman*. Yes, Hollywood was sort of the musical comedy version of Cedar Rapids.

RKO was so desperate it gave Welles carte blanche (French for "Kiss my ass") control over whatever he wanted to do. According to the sweetest film contract since Chuck Chaplin and

---

[4] Does he expect tough sledding . . .? Sorry, the author apologizes for succumbing to this cheap pun, but it's an overgrowth of having done the Marx Brothers *Duck Soup* chapter.

116

some friends formed their own studio, Welles wasn't even required to show RKO his daily rushes. This was unprecedented stuff, and Hollywood (the original source of both sin and sixty-six forms of jealousy) had a collective shit-fit. In the film industry you were supposed to pay your dues, and even then nobody was allowed to have that much in-your-face power.

No less a talent than novelist F. Scott Fitzgerald (someone who'd paid his film dues but still didn't get to sit at the adult table) cruelly observed, "All's well that ends well(es)." And it was a crack that spoke for most of the film capital, that sunny place for shady people. Even when Welles tried to indirectly address the situation, like growing a beard to look older, Hollywood gave no quarter. They claimed he was assuming an artsy fartsy pose and continued to say things about his mother.

There were, however, some Hollywood insiders who gave tips (other than get out of town) to Welles. Of course they were heavily disguised and/or hiding behind bushes, but they tried. For example, John Ford helped, and Welles screened the celebrated director's then contemporary *Stagecoach* just under a million times. Welles would later say he studied Hollywood's old masters, "By which I mean, John Ford, John Ford, and John Ford."[5] The great cinematographer Gregg Toland gave Welles a crash course on photography and later was behind the camera on *Citizen Kane*.[6] Fittingly, Welles always claimed being a film novice was a great advantage, meaning he was too dumb to realize certain things

---

[5] Ford was also helpful in other ways. When he came on the *Citizen Kane* set to wish the young director luck he spotted an informer for an anti-Welles faction among the crew. With his comic Irish directness, Ford greeted the man, "Well, well, how's old snake-in-the grass Eddie?"

[6] They got along so well they planned to film the life story of Christ next, with Welles in the lead. But it never happened. Maybe they couldn't get clearance.

Sadly, Welles was a has-been by the time he died, a mere shadow -- although a large one -- of his younger self. (Welles trying to look older just prior to shooting *Citizen Kane*.)

were supposed to be impossible. But this "innocence is better" philosophy only bunched up Hollywood's collective panties all the more. As Walter Winchell once said, or maybe it was my barber, "Hollywood is a place where they shoot too many pictures and not enough actors."

Like most of Welles' subsequent films, *Citizen Kane* was about the fall from power of a great man, or at least one who thought he was pretty great. After the opening *Rosebud* death scene (for now just think sled and not other forms of sliding), Welles hits the viewer with a loud, brassy "March of Time" type newsreel that gives you a quick and dirty overview of Kane. We learn the old moneybags was into collecting "the loot of the world" and that he had "the biggest private zoo since Noah."

While these are, of course, fascinating facts . . . not, the real movie starts with the decision to have a reporter define Kane by tracking down the meaning of *Rosebud*. Gee, this was a rather Freudian journalist, don't you think? Anyway, several prominent people in the late, great Kane's life are uncovered.

The first is Mr. Thatcher (George Coulouris) the banker who became Kane's guardian when the boy inherited a trillion dollars and change and was taken from his parents. We learn the least from him, because unlike the other pivotal Kane connections, Thatcher is dead, which always lessens the chance of a good interview. Yet it is consistent with his coldness, even in life. Fittingly, the reporter learns Thatcher's views by visiting a crypt-like archive housing his memoirs. [7] This takes the viewer into a flashback where Kane is seen as a boy playing with his sled – gosh, imagine that. One squints hard to spot a name on the sled but there is always strategically placed snow covering it.

---

[7] Not once during the whole *Rosebud* search are we allowed to see the reporter's face. This keeps things focused on the mystery of *Rosebud* . . . and saves money on casting.

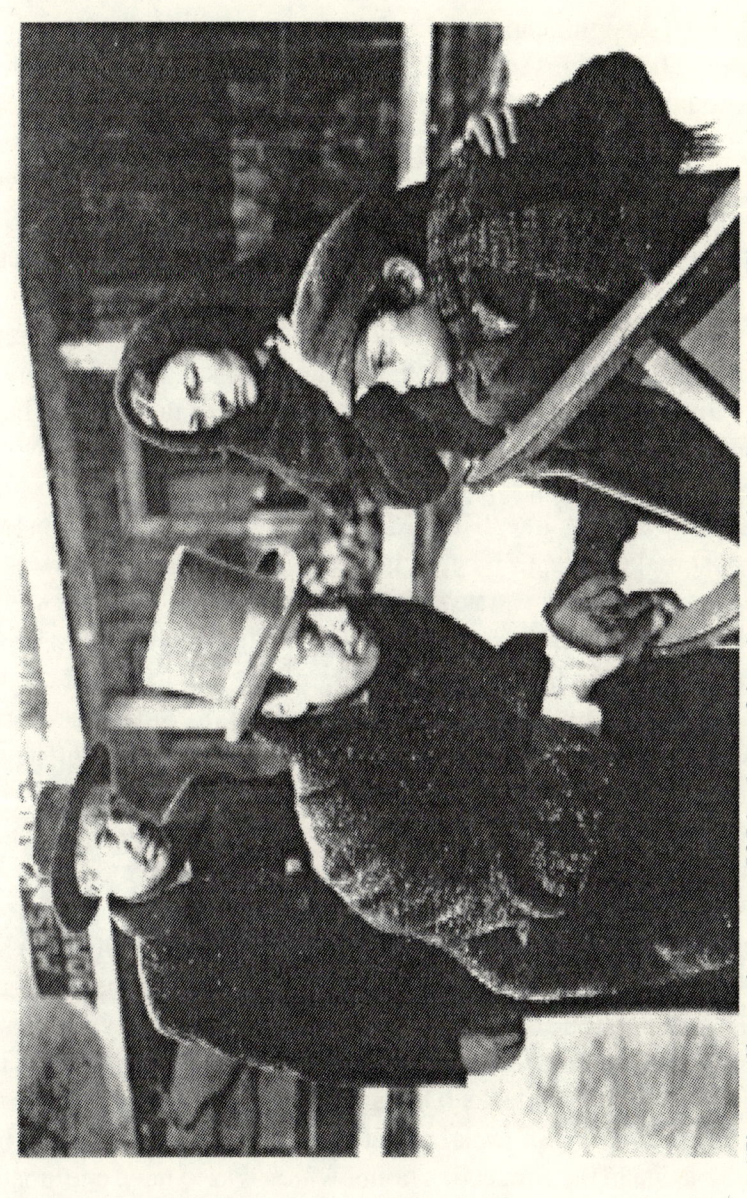

"I'm really a nice guy. If I had any friends you could ask them." (Icy Thatcher tries to get chummy with the young Kane in *Citizen Kane* -- that's Rosebud on the right.)

The significance of the sled is fleetingly established in three ways. The kid tries to brain Thatcher with it when he realizes he's being taken away. Then, the sled is the last thing seen as the boy exits the only real home he'll ever know. And on Kane's first Christmas away Thatcher attempts to suck up by gifting him with another sled. But the child gives Thatcher this withering look, as if to say, "Bite me, Old Man." (Yes, it's easy to see why this is the greatest sled movie ever made.)

The flashback via Thatcher's memoirs then jumps to Kane's early adulthood and the still ongoing antagonism between the two. For instance, Thatcher, the least spontaneous of men, nearly has a stroke when the young Kane cavalierly writes him, "I think it would be fun to run a newspaper." One half expects Thatcher to blurt out some epithet, like "Holy Mary, Mother of God." But instead he just makes like he'll be giving off steam any second now.

Later, after the newspaper suffers huge losses, he warns Kane this can't continue, to which the manchild replies, "You know, Mr. Thatcher, at the rate of losing a million dollars a year . . . I'll have to close this place in fifty or sixty years." Smart ass cracks like that make the titanic egomaniac revealed in the opening news-reel seem rather likable. After all, who can't relate to screwing the authority figures of the world. Now, if Welles had only said it while in Groucho makeup it would have been perfect.

The reporter next tracks down the first living witness, Kane's business manager Bernstein (Everett Sloan). Since he has forever idolized Kane, is there any question the lionizing of the man will continue during this segment? Consequently, he relates how Kane assembled New York's finest staff of journalists at his paper and even drafted a "Declaration of Principles," which will of course make him look bad later in the picture. There's a big party scene in the film at this point, which was to have culminated in a trip to a brothel, always a nice festive idea for males in the audience. But Welles cut it because he was such a Puritan. Yeah right. Actually, he knew the censorship people would have gone scissor happy, so he saved them the trouble. Still, it is a pity, because to party retards the aging process . . . well, it retards something.

The only thing even mildly negative about Kane in the Thatcher-Bernstein segments concerns the Spanish American War. Borrowing an anecdote sometimes attributed to Hearst, Kane wires a conscientious reporter in Cuba unable to find any sign of conflict, "You provide me prose poems and I'll provide the war." Ok, ok, it's a classic case of the dreaded *Yellow Journalism*. But Welles manages to carry the scene off with a youthful charismatic spirit, not unlike Bonnie and Clyde knocking over another bank. Oh, it's not right but everyone occasionally feels the desire to do whatever he wants, even if it's nothing more than just drop-kicking your neighbor's brattin' kid into another county.

The next historical witness, Kane's one-time best friend Jed Leland (Joseph Cotton), is the tattletale type. From this point on in the film one gets the idea that if Kane is the answer, it must be a very peculiar question. Leland begins with the unraveling of Kane's first marriage to Emily Norton (Ruth Warrick). This flashback contains the famous breakfast sequence, where a series of dissolves through the years documents the originally kissy face relationships of Kane and Emily going into the dumpster.

Through the years they get progressively further apart physically at breakfast, while their dialogues get increasingly harsher, culminating in his interruption and completion of her statement, "'People will think' . . . 'what I tell them to think.'" This mutual partnership ends with her being the mute, though she lands a great visual jab by eventually reading a rival newspaper at the table. It was your basic All-American dysfunctional family (wouldn't it be great if insecurity and desperation made us more attractive.)

Soon Kane takes a mistress[8], Susan Alexander (Dorothy

---

[8] Period comic Joe E. Lewis coined this definition of a mistress, "Something that goes between mister and mattress."

Comingore), who was not exactly an idiot but she had more than a touch of it. There's no accounting for taste. But Kane was moved by the fact she initially liked him despite not knowing what an important person he was. Of course, Susan was so dumb it's questionable whether she knew who *she* was. When the relationship is eventually revealed, with the accompanying scandal (as always happens, at least in Hollywood), it ends both his marriage and a promising political career. The ugly but impressive close to this chapter has Kane angrily screaming and pursuing his political rival down a huge winding staircase. With Kane, as with many people, it is sometimes hard to see the good . . . especially when it doesn't seem to be there. [9]

The cluck named Susan goes on to be the second Mrs. Kane. And because the press questioned the talents of his aspiring singer/wife, Kane builds Susan an opera house for her high art debut. If he cannot be elected to public office, he will make something of this protégé. Wrong. It's not even close. Susan's voice is somewhere between Yoko Ono's and a cat in a blender. Indeed, the actress playing Susan couldn't make her voice bad enough so a professional no talent was hired (how'd you like that on your business card?) and her unmelodious warblings were dubbed in. They say it isn't over until the fat lady sings. But when Susan opened her mouth it was more like the fat lady and all her fat pals were singing, and it was a regular polka . . . never a good sign.

This performance from hell received reviews to match, including in Kane's paper. [10] Former buddy Leland was the drama

---

[9] Welles so threw himself into the staircase scene he did a two-and-a-half gainer down the steps and messed up his ankle. Hollywood joked about his ego going unscathed.

[10] In depression America the opera was a popular way to lampoon the misplaced values of the rich. The Marx Brothers had already devoted a whole movie to derailing high society in just that manner – *A Night at the Opera*. Unfortunately, the Marxes weren't available to Welles.

critic. But he had to get soused to even face his typewriter. Two damning sentences into the critique, whiskey coma took over. Kane found Leland snoozing and out of some prick of conscience (which is also how he would have defined Leland) Kane ghosted the rest of the review in that spirit.

When Leland wakes up (you can only sleep on a typewriter so long), he wanders over to the still-typing Kane. The two had had a falling out months before over the scandal. And now Leland says, "Hello Charlie – I didn't know we were speaking."

Kane replies without turning, "Sure we're speaking, Jed; you're fired." This sort of dampened any chance of a reconciliation. But Kane would suffer a delayed double whammy over the incident. First, Susan took Kane's head off about being trashed in his own paper. And if you thought her screeching opera voice was bad (actually no thinking was required on that one, even for the hearing impaired), Susan's ticked-out-of-her-mind screeching rampage had dogs six states away scrambling for ear plugs.

Interestingly enough, Welles' only later regret about making *Citizen Kane* was portraying the mistress as such a no-talent. Hearst's real sweetie (Marion Davies) was a gifted comic actress, though understandably humor impaired when it came to the figure of Susan Alexander. Regardless, this shows a nice spirit on Welles' part. Plus, artistic *angst* always plays well with the critics.

Returning to *Citizen Kane*, Leland sends Kane the original draft of the publisher's "Declaration of Principles," something Kane had not been practicing for some time. (Leland had built up an animosity that can only be explained by Jung and Freud combined.) Anyway, the "Declaration of Principles" doesn't change Kane (it is easier and so much more fun to just be nasty) but it put a severe crimp in his day. There's nothing worse than a friend who plays conscience . . . or who has kids that play piano.

While the Leland showcased in these flashbacks makes

the behavior of your standard wet blanket seem like a television evangelist on shore leave, whenever the film comes back to the reporter and the now elderly, nursing home bound Leland, he is the most entertaining of the people interviewed. For instance, he observes, "You know when I was a young man, there was an impression around that nurses were pretty. It was no truer than it is now." Ok, so it's not exactly Robin Williams. But in a film this dark you learn to savor even chuckles.

Of course, at one point Welles had planned to comically punch things up. For instance, in the original script he had flirted with giving Leland a reoccurring fantasy, where he worked in a deli. And each day a beautiful girl named *Rosebud* came in and asked for a pound of tongue. But every time he said, "I get off at six," her response was always the same, "I never get off; that's why I want a pound of tongue."

Anyway, Leland's levity seems all the more pointed when our *Rosebud* reporter interviews the second Mrs. Kane – Susan "Dragon Lady" Alexander, who has gone from opera screecher to nightclub screecher. It's no improvement, but at least the latter audience can defend themselves by getting stinko drunk. Susan, who is shellacked herself during the interview, is currently entertaining (the word is used loosely) in a real dive, sort of an ashtray with music. Her flashback memories find Kane as a cross between Darth Vader and Freddy Krueger. After her hello-I-must-be-going diva debut, she got the brainstorm that maybe opera was not her thing. But Kane kept pushing her to perform and finally Susan decides to join her ancestors, a fate critics had been hoping for since that opening.

Anyhow, in keeping with her putz of the century credentials, she's a big floperoo in her own attempted suicide. Kane's discovery of the drug overdosed Susan is one of the film's most celebrated scenes, since no one wants to see her sorry butt of a character ever again. Well, ok, maybe this is a bit of an overstatement but today's audience frequently does break into spontaneous applause and whistles when they think she's history. Maybe that's not particularly nice, but the woman's voice would have pissed-off Mother Teresa, or the contemporary saint of your choice.

Film texts, however, highlight this scene because it was shot in deep focus, a technique rarely used before. [11] Traditionally, the scene would have opened with a shot of an empty pill box, followed by a cut to the passed out Ms. Screecher (unusual in that her trap is shut), followed by a cut to macho man Kane breaking down the locked door. You know, spoon feeding by the editor – look here, look there . . . with deep focus (they call it that because they had to call it something) there's no editing and the viewer can pick whatever he or she wants to look at in the film frames . . . unless there's some heavy making out going on with your date. In that case, the intellectual excitement associated with deep focus pales considerably, and one's main concern should be with trying to get up off that sticky floor with some dignity, as well as not spilling the popcorn.

The rest of Susan's sequence is how Kane built this castle of a home for her called Xanadu. [12] (The real Hearst palace was once described by Shaw as the kind of place God would have had, if He'd had the money.) But in the movie it was really more of a prison with room service. Isolated on a huge estate Susan described as "40,000 acres of scenery," she eventually walks out on Kane. All-powerful types do not take rejection well, especially when it involves their main squeeze. Thus, in another memorable moment from the movie, Kane does one of the best room trashing

---

[11] For an in-depth look at this overrated phenomenon either go to grad school, or read any of those "cinema" critics who always use the word mise-en-scene. This author is busy at the moment.

[12] Xanadu should not be confused with the Olivia Newton-John musical of the same name – a movie so bad it makes the film *Truck Stop Women of the Moon* seem like a classic.

scenes this side of Martin Sheen in *Apocalypse Now*. And like Sheen, Welles also put a major gash in one of his hands during the shooting of the sequence. When later asked what was going through his mind during this famous scene, Welles said "As a bleeder, I was just trying to not pass out."

The reporter's final interview is with Kane's butler Raymond (Paul Stewart), a man with all the warmth and personality of a side of beef. He adds little, other than noting Kane had said *Rosebud* once before, just at the close of trashing Susan's room. Kane had happened upon her glass ball with the snow scene inside. You know, those paperweights you shake and it looks like it's snowing inside, unless yours has a defective seal and then it just leaks down your pants leg. This was the same ball Kane had been holding on his death bed, way back at the start of the movie, when he also blurted out *Rosebud*, obviously, you don't need to be a shrink to figure – snow . . . sled . . . childhood . . . latent homosexual . . . oops, wrong chart. Anyway, with the torching of the sled, that's Kane's story.

Audiences in 1941 weren't yet ready for heroes with clay feet, as in depressing stuff. This was the same year Gary Cooper got an Oscar for *Sergeant York* – a good traditional American war hero – a religious farm boy who learns killing German soldiers can be fun too. Neither could period audiences appreciate the tragic overtones of Kane's life.[13] The American dream was still box-office.[14] Sure, Kane dared to be too big, but that's what made him both fascinating and doomed to failure.

---

[13] Of course, today's mass audience isn't exactly demanding the film be re-released either, unless maybe some dinosaur sequences could be added.

[14] Welles' thoughts on the American dream might be capsulized to a comment he made to actress Cybill Shepherd years later, "Everything you ever learned in school is balls!"

Welles would never again have this kind of power on a picture. Conservative Hollywood was dancing in the streets. The boy genius would never again equal what is now considered the greatest film ever made. [15] Before he was thirty Welles was being called America's youngest living has-been (ouch). But hey, even if he never bettered *Citizen Kane*, look around; no one else has either.

---

[15] Some *Touch of Evil* fanatics will contest this, but just ignore them. They're harmless.

High Noon's Gary Cooper, Grandfather
clock's stand-in, and some Quaker.

HIGH NOON

Unlike the early "Adult Western," where the hero
loves his horse more than the heroine but he's
worried about it, for most of *High Noon* hero Gary
Cooper has neither a horse nor a heroine.

High Noon is *the* Western for many people, especially those able
to handle Tex Ritter singing "Do Not Forsake Me, Oh My Darlin'"
just over six million times. [1] This was the first Western to really
use (rhymes with abuse) the theme song. Of course, this is pre-
Frankie Laine – the Western singer who was sort of a cross between William Bendix and a Flintstone vitamin.

It was a groundbreaking film in three additional ways. The
story is told in "real time," with the action meant to take place in
just under 90 minutes. Thus, the filmmakers show you the grandfather clock in the town's hotel lobby every 3.2 seconds. One
sees so much of it during *High Noon* (the grandfather clock received second billing behind Gary Cooper) that it later had a strong
supporting role in the hit TV program *Captain Kangaroo*.

Second, instead of the typical Western populism, where
people are always good and helpful, the *High Noon* folks have no
time to assist Cooper's sheriff. Now there's a good reason for
this – bad man F-R-A-N-K M-I-L-L-E-R ! (Ian MacDonald) –
has just been paroled from prison and he is gunning for Marshall

---

[1] The song was later used as a form of punishment in many marriage encounter sessions. The number of times one heard the
ballad in *High Noon* was cut after a preview audience nearly had
a laughing fit. Unfortunately, no more material about this was
available. Sorry.

Coop, "The man what sent me up." (Remedial English had not yet caught on in the West.) It kind of makes you think Darwin might have been wrong.

Anyway, whenever the name Frank Miller comes up conversations stop and people soil themselves. Like a lot of murderous types, he is sometimes called a "loner." Naturally Miller was a loner, he killed every cowboy in sight. But on this occasion he was being joined by additional bad men – hardly an effective selling point when recruiting deputies. Regardless, Miller was coming into town on the *noon* train and planned to send Cooper, and anyone with him, to cowboy heaven.

Consequently, when our hero asks for support, people claim they want to help but the alibis include everything from "My guns are in the shop," to the ever popular: "We've already been to three shootouts this week." Yes, there's nothing like imminent death to put a crimp in the reliability of friends.

The third bit of western revisionism [2] involves our hero. While most six-gun stories paint a picture of romantic heroism, Gary Cooper's character represents a de-glamorized look at the town marshal. Translation: the guy's scared shitless. Yes, he acts like a gang of gay cowboys has broken into his jail and redecorated it. Granted, this is still Gary tall-in-the-saddle Cooper. We know he will do the right thing. They wouldn't have given the Best Actor Oscar for the role if he were a total chicken.

Cooper's characterization is not without the psychology of fear, versus, say Alan Ladd's title role the following year in *Shane*. Coop masterfully wove strength and vulnerability in the fabric of his portrayal of the sheriff. In contrast, Ladd had so many mythic dimensions it merely seems as if he is slumming on earth from a cowboy Mount Olympus. And while "golden-boy" Ladd looks like he's about six-years-old, Cooper appears hag-

---

[2] This is a sixty-dollar word meaning to "break the rules."

gard and old, half-past a hundred, like a cowboy vampire on a day pass. Of course, while facing death doesn't exactly give you a perky look, the sheriff is aging faster than that picture in Dorian Gray's closet.

Cooper has, moreover, the added problem that his new bride, Princess Grace [3] – I mean, Grace Kelly – is a Quaker, opposed to violence, especially the kind involving guns and lead poisoning. Obviously no one had told her that in the Old West gunpowder represented a kind of insecticide for pesky humans. Regardless, everyone knows violence is as American as apple pie.

Unlike what we now know about the real Kelly, who was as pure as the driven snow until she drifted (rim shot, her *High Noon* character comes across as a professional virgin.) And like a Woody Allen character, she finds it hard to get her heart and head together at the same time. In fact, they are not even friendly. Consequently, when Cooper decides he must fight, she basically tells him to eat shit and die.

Kelly does, however, represent a very traditional character in the Western: the ball-buster blonde WASP/school teacher type who symbolized the eastern civilization which will eventually tame the West (no shooting after 5 o'clock), whether it wants to be tamed or not. Yes, there was just a tad of racism in the genre. Especially since the standard cowboy hero's first girlfriend is invariably of ethnic saloon girl background. Fittingly, before Kelly, Cooper had been involved with the worldly (read sexy) Mexican saloon owner Helen Ramirez (Katy Jurado). But tsk, tsk, we must not have any threat of mixing the races. Ramirez does, however, escape with her life. In many classic Aryan Westerns, like director John (cowboy hats off in respect) Ford's *My Darling Clementine*, the Mexican saloon girl/love interest buys

---

[3] Grace Kelly later married Prince Rainier of Monaco, a country so small she later had it carpeted.

the farm. Needless to say, knocking her off takes the stress out of choosing the WASP.

Naturally, the standard saloon girl, regardless of race, was always ultimately off-limits for marriage. This is because in the Old West, "saloon girl" was a euphemism for, if you'll excuse the expression, "whore." You know, as in – save a horse, ride a cowboy. That's why Matt Dillon never married Miss Kitty (the name makes more sense now, doesn't it?) on *Gunsmoke*. It wasn't called TV's first "Adult Western" for nothing. Didn't you ever wonder about all those rooms above the Long Branch Saloon? Get with the program. Anyway, since novelist Owen Wister's celebrated Western *The Virginian* [4] which introduced such classic tough cowboy lines as "Smile when you say that," the genre has often featured a goody-goody pacifist heroine like Kelly. [5]

Before tracing the individual stories of betrayal by Cooper's *High Noon* loosely-labeled "friends," one needs to add a reference to the 1950's Cold War and Joseph "Commie witch-hunting" McCarthy. Yes, you heard "right." *High Noon* was made at a time when everyone in America but Edward R. Murrow and a longshoreman named Guido were afraid to clear their throats for fear of being branded a communist. Period critics saw the film's hypocritical, non-helping townspeople as a reflection of then contemporary America.

Now before you make some rash crack about critics, the *High Noon*-McCarthy connection had real credence. The film's screenwriter, Carl Foreman, later admitted he had penned it as an allegory of the blacklisting fear then gripping Hollywood. Indeed, the town's fictional name of "Hadleyville" was used to sug-

---

[4] The book was dedicated to Wister's buddy, Rough and Ready Teddy Roosevelt, America's only president to actually think of himself as a cowboy.

[5] Prolonged exposure to Kelly's character has produced diabetes in laboratory cowboys.

gest Hollywood. Foreman's insights were rewarded in period style . . . he was later blacklisted.

The allegorical slant, however, can become more convoluted. Swedish film critics of the 1950's liked the *High Noon*-McCarthy interpretation so much that if they had had tails they would have been wagging. Plus, they saw this Western as a reflection of America's then current involvement in Korea, with little or no assistance from other nations. While it is swell of Swedish critics to critique American Westerns, they were probably just killing time until Ingmar Bergman became big. Swedes do much better with solitude, religious pain, and those little meatballs.

Meanwhile, back at *High Noon*'s ticking clock, Cooper continues to look for help without once thinking of the Yellow Pages. But the search provides the opportunity for several cameo appearances by prominent character actors willing to be remembered as cowardly weasels for the rest of whatever. The most striking chicken is Harry Morgan, later famous for his Colonel Potter role on TV's *M.A.S.H.*. In *High Noon* he cannot even face Cooper, sending his wife to the door while he hides under the bed. But Morgan probably would not have been able to provide much assistance anyway. His character looks like the meanest thing he ever did was ring somebody's doorbell and run. Through the years Morgan has popped up in several classic Westerns, such as Henry Fonda's buddy in *The Ox-Bow Incident* and the sheriff afraid of John Wayne in *The Shootist*. However, Morgan's realistic weenie of a friend in *High Noon* is the ultimate justification for becoming a recluse and changing your name to milquetoast. As with most scaredy-cats, he thinks with his feet.

Another notable cameo appearance is by Lon Chaney, Jr. – who plays the town's retired sheriff. If he doesn't look quite right as a Geritol gunslinger, it is because he was forever typecast earlier as Hollywood's favorite hairy monster in *The Wolf Man*, *Wolf Man Meets the Space Monster*, *Wolf Man Marries Jesse James' Daughter* . . ..

Instead of turning him into an old cowboy, the *High Noon* producers should have made him up one more time as a werewolf. Just think what a *revisionist* Western that would have been. One conscientious werewolf has got to be equal to the biggest posse this side of central casting. Since very few cowboys packed silver bullets (barring an appearance by the Lone Ranger), nobody could have brought Lon "Wolf Man" Chaney down. They might have even beefed up the title as something like, *The Good, The Bad, and The Wolf Man*.

Chaney had the best excuse for not helping out – rheumatism, always a bummer if you're trying to do that quick draw stuff. But his key reason for not assisting Coop was well put – the hypocritical townspeople are not worth it:

> People gotta talk themselves into law and order
> before they do anything about it. Maybe because
> down deep they don't care. They just don't care.

Pretty articulate for a fellow (Chaney) also associated with playing Lenny from *Of Mice and Men*.

Chaney's two-faced slant on the people was further articulated by *High Noon*'s cowardly judge (Otto Kruger). Best known for his earlier film roles as the smooth, cynical villain, such as his Nazi parts in *Hitler's Children* (better than the title sounds – well, not that much better) and Hitchcock's *Saboteur*, the history lesson he gives Cooper's marshal is a further summing up of Wolf Man Chaney's argument that the townspeople are not worth saving. And if a werewolf would have been *frightfully* helpful to Cooper, adding a Nazi or two couldn't have hurt.

Sure, sure, Nazis in the Old West would have been a bit of an anachronism, especially if they were driving their goofy-look-

"I'm so mad I could stomp bunnies."
(Lon Chaney, Jr. in *The Wolf Man* --
potentially one scary cowboy.)

136

ing early Volkswagen Beetle prototypes.[6] Regardless, a good scriptwriter could have set up a plot twist to get some Nazis into *High Noon*. For instance, several 19th century American Indian tribes used the swastika as a mystic sign. Thus, why not goosestep genealogical storm troopers into the Old West via a time warp, sort of a *Nazis Back to the Future*. However it is done, the bottom line is that Nazis are box office. That's why they were reintroduced in the third Indiana Jones film. Free historical footnote: The two most written about figures in Western culture are Jesus Christ and Adolph Hitler.[7] Not exactly your most logical double date duo. Evil has some sort of macabre fascination, as long as it is not being done to you.

High Noon's biggest supporting player betrayal of Cooper, since Hitler was never worked into the story, comes at the hands of the film's best known character actor – *Thomas Mitchell*. He had earlier won rave reviews and an Oscar for his alcohol-soaked geezer Doc Boone in another celebrated Western, John Ford's *Stagecoach*. In this film Mitchell battled small town hypocrisy when he wasn't battling whiskey coma. He also surfaced as the most likeable of characters in such "Capra-corn" classics as *Mr. Smith Goes to Washington* (Mitchell was a hard-drinking reporter; gee, there's an original characterization) and *It's a Wonderful Life* (as the pleasantly daffy Uncle Billy . . . or was he just "stewed"?)

In *High Noon* he plays Cooper's best friend . . . until he

---

[6] Still, it wouldn't have been any worse than that geekie jeep Roy Rogers' TV bubba sidekick Pat Brady had. Named "Nellybelle," it used to drive the discerning 1950's kid viewer up the wall; even the peewee critic recognized basic Western genre conventions, such as *no jeeps, please!*

[7] Third Reich scholars have recently made a remarkable discovery about Hitler's childhood. It seems he tied his shoelaces into little knotties.

inexplicably turns on him. Mitchell is in the town church giving what seems to be your standard populist "win one for the Gipper" speech. Well, since you have heard this a cazillion times in other Westerns, your mind (assuming you have one) starts to wander, especially with Mitchell's character always coming through in earlier pictures. After all, you don't star in Ford and Capra films without being a real mensch. Ah, but here is where that nasty phenomenon called "casting against type" sneaks in. A performer establishes a specific character reputation fans enjoy and then, for some perverse reason (plus a sackfull of money), he/she turns on you.

Mitchell's *High Noon* figure suddenly, in mid-speech, becomes a Jekyll & Hyde, convincing the church crowd (not that these born-again chickens needed much convincing) it would be in everyone's best interest not to help the marshal. Other than Cooper's sweetie leaving him, Mitchell's betrayal is the hardest for the sheriff to take. And of course, it is frustrating for the viewer because one second you're listening to an old populist pitch (with your eyes beginning to glaze over for just a second) and the next thing you know, Mr. Dependable has kicked Cooper in his privates, metaphorically.

The marshal also catches it from these holy rollers for not attending church regularly. The man was definitely not having a nice day, especially with his next church visit threatening to be in a pine box.

For the student of *High Noon*, the most interesting thing about the movie is how it was saved after some disastrous preview. Yes, this certified classic was initially perceived as a real bow-wow, or as the Hollywood saying goes, "The producers knew they had heard the turkey's gobble." The audience rating cards said things like, "we wish you would have forgotten to put film in the camera," and "why don't you just stop the projector and tell the people a terrible mistake has been made." The bottom line (accent on bottom) was the movie had no dramatic tension, and

Grace Kelly couldn't act her way out of a monogrammed paper sack. Oh, she showed promise, just not in the movies. What to do, then, with this clunker?

Kelly's part was edited down to a minimum, making her yet another beautiful face on the industry's proverbial cutting room floor. For tension, the film's real time factor was enhanced, with the role of the clock being beefed up, meaning lots of ticking inserts. And believe it or not, Tex Ritter's warbling of "Do Not Forsake Me, Oh My Darlin'" was added . . . and added . . . and added. . ..

To enhance Cooper's screen "angst," *High Noon* footage of his performance initially discarded was reinstated. That is, the actor had been in poor physical health during the shooting of the film, and both his personal life and career were hurting. Thus, he was not a happy cowpoke, and it showed. But as one of the definitive all-American nice guys, production people had protected how this movie icon appeared on the screen. (This is also known as sucking-up, big time). As an attempt was made, however, to save the film, it was decided the painful-looking footage of Cooper was more in keeping with what was happening to his character.

After all, nine out of ten marshals facing death alone, abandoned by everyone, not to mention an (as one critic put it) "unravished bride," would tend to look pained, even downright grumpy. And it worked. Critics ate up his "performance." Cooper, never a fan of method actors (he called them a "bunch of goofballs"), would seem to have inadvertently benefited from this approach in *High Noon*. Or perhaps, as *the* method guru Lee Strasberg once suggested of Cooper's career in general, he was just a natural method actor who didn't know it.

Everyone seems to have their favorite *High Noon* part, though many viewers are just happy when it gets to be twelve o'clock and they can stop looking at the damn clock. But probably the biggest audience reaction occurs when Grace Kelly's character decides to help her husband after all and blows away one of the gang and later distracts M-I-L-L-E-R so her hubby can plug him. Being a Quaker and all, Kelly is not well-versed in violence, yet she takes to it, *royally*. Being no fool, though her SAT scores weren't all that hot, Kelly's blasting of one heavy in the *back* gave a whole new slant to that old axiom, "behind every man . . .. "

Another popular scene is the livery stable fistfight between Cooper's sheriff and his former deputy Harv (Lloyd Bridges), who would like the marshal to leave so he can go for a promotion. Their physical battle is interesting because Cooper does not win easily, nor does he look particularly pretty when it is over – a refreshing twist from the period's traditional Western where the hero could take on the entire Sioux nation and not even muss his hair.

Unfortunately, fans of 1950's television are now distracted by Bridges' casting, due to his hit series *Sea Hunt*, where he spent more time underwater than Flipper. This strong ongoing identification with the world of snorkeling makes Bridges in a cowboy outfit a real hoot. [8]

As a special historical footnote, brought to you at no extra charge, Bridges' presence in *High Noon* is now also distracting from a political perspective. Earlier in the chapter (no fair peeking) this film was described as a liberal attack on McCarthy America. Ironically, Bridges was later a key friendly witness in the second round of House Un-American Activities Committee hearings. Go figure.

Ok, ok, Cooper is sometimes also listed as a friendly wit-

---

[8] If one could anticipate things like this, the problem might have been corrected by giving the film a slight Jacques Cousteau twist. And the people in publicity would have loved saloon girls in swimsuits. Moreover, it might have given "Hollywood's Mermaid," Esther Williams, a new '50s career direction, such as *High Noon in Malibu*, or *Neptune's Daughter Meets Billy The Kid*.

ness but when you go through his testimony (bring lots of coffee) he comes off as a wise fool. The man is cordial but claims ignorance on so many questions from the HUAC that, unless he had just recently had a lobotomy, it now sounds as if Cooper is politely jerking the members around.

Without trying to belabor the issue, the McCarthy connection remains an important part of the film's history. It went beyond political position, whether right, left, or in the middle with the covers pulled over your head. That is, some 1950's western purists felt no political perspective should be added. [9] More specifically, it was argued that the traditional Western hero neither asked for nor needed help from any of the wimps in town.

Director Howard Hawks would later film *Rio Bravo* as an answer to *High Noon*. The movie showcased John Wayne (who had tamed the West single-handedly several times already – just see his filmography) as another beleaguered sheriff. But does he ask for help? All together now: "N-O!" The only assistance he receives is a further comic commentary on the Western hero's independence, since his sidekicks all have some potentially fatal flaws, from method drinker Dean Martin's alcoholic character to Walter Brennan's old geezer with the gimpy leg and no teeth.

Despite such detractors, *High Noon* remains a frequently revived classic which has influenced countless Westerns, such as Clint Eastwood's Gothic slant on the genre, *High Plains Drifter*. In this movie revenge is taken against another chicken town for its desertion of a sheriff. But unlike *High Noon*'s Cooper, who gets to win, throw down his badge, and ride off with a future princess, the *High Plains Drifter* marshal bites the bullet early, and Eastwood's mysterious stranger (possibly the ghost of this

---

[9] Recent research has revealed these are the same people who as children forever threatened to take their ball and bat home if they do not get their way.

sheriff-boogie, boogie) gets to play avenger, appointing a dwarf as mayor and eventually burning the town down.

Like Mark Twain's short story "The Man That Corrupted Hadleyburg," *High Noon*'s Hadleyville is a town of smug religious hypocrites just waiting to be derailed (tarred and feathered would also be a nice period punishment). For that reason alone, not to mention Gary "He's Our Hero" Cooper coming through, this movie will remain a lesson against such two-faced "folks," as well as an explanation as to why Cooper's marshal is not a regular at church. In fact, like many Western lawmen, he was a *paranoid agnostic*. He doubts the existence of God yet believes there's some force out there screwing him over.

"Sure, Nosferatu, anybody can have bad breath
but yours could knock a buzzard off a shit wagon."

(Max Schreck's title vampire in the original *Nosferatu* has no direct tie-in with the text but an exception was made given that this
is the goofiest still we've ever seen.)

AFTERWORD

Call me crazy (oh, go ahead; you'll feel better) but this spoof book will generate a lot of discussion, some intelligent, some critical. Thus, because all the best texts have these closing remarks, an *Afterword* has been added. It also allows the reader to feel he or she is getting something extra, always an effective marketing scam. Plus, it is an easy catchall for things the author forgot to mention earlier but doesn't want to work too hard adding now. Writers are, after all, as lazy as the next person. We just *seem* more industrious since we save every good phrase – and those of anyone who happens to be passing by the word processor – and put them between two covers. We're essentially *word thiefs*. But enough about trade secrets.

Anyhow, *The Seventh Seal* chapter (as good as it is [1]) might have included more background on just what Judgement Day catastrophes (besides parking and the high cost of sinning) are prophesized in the symbolic seven seals of the zany book called *Revelations*. (This is the one section of the *Bible* scholars think was written on acid, or at least on some very good mushrooms.)

These apocalyptic warnings include the ever popular wars across the land, your basic hellfire (which has been the most publicized), that inseparable duo famine and pestilence, the occasional earthquake, the always attention-getting blackening of the sun (except for L.A. residents), more frogs and locusts than you could shake a stick at (if you find that entertaining), single lane traffic during rush hour, and the moon turning the color of blood – never a good sign, especially if you've been bad or you're a little sketchy on just what your good qualities are.

Once the final or seventh seal has been opened and all these events occur (plus a few more we're not allowed to disclose at this time), then things are really going to get bad. You don't

---

[1] Feel free to look it over again.

want to know. We're talking major, *major* bad day. But there will be (according to scripture, and the ouija board which came with my Chevy) 144,000 holy rollers spared the eternal damnation of hell and other unpleasant experiences. Crosses will appear on the foreheads of these goody goodies (honest). But it's not clear from the original text (especially if, like me, your Hebrew is not quite what it used to be), whether these crosses will be visible to the *naked* eye – if that phrase is still permissible – or if they will appear only under some sort of heavenly black light.

Along similar catch-up lines, I also feel a need to add an addendum to the *Psycho* chapter. Work, work, work. The only flaw in that picture (Hitchcock purists best cover their ears) is a general lack of information as to why Nutty Norman (Anthony Perkins) jumped the tracks. Well, your sick prayers are answered in *Psycho IV*, as well as bringing back Perkins and scriptwriter Joseph Stefano, who adapted the original novel for Hitchcock.

Psycho IV finds a cured Bates (yeah, right) calling a talk show and discussing his past, with flashbacks – gotta have that now in color blood, no more of Hitch's substitute chocolate syrup. The radio program's topic is "boys who have killed their mother," always a popular easy listening subject. And Perkins' old Norman is in all his glory, or is that *gory*. He recalls a childhood (more flashbacks) where his mother is a major loon, too. Played by a sexy Olivia Hussey (accent on that last name), she is all grown-up from her late 1960s career breakthrough in *Romeo and Juliet*.

Written along slutty lines, Hussey brings a wonderful bitchiness to the role, possibly from being pissed over falling from Shakespeare to *Psycho IV* . . . for cable, no less. Anyway, her carnal tendencies gave poor Normy mixed messages about what it meant to *love* one's mummy. Still, the boy might have coped had she not married a mean spirited muttonhead. Young Norman wasn't going to be replaced.

Not surprisingly, *Psycho IV* shows him flirting with murder one more time. But thankfully for the hotel trade, not to mention shower curtain manufacturers everywhere, Norman falls in love with his shrink, a woman whose post-graduate study was probably entitled "Playing Russian Roulette for Fun and Profit," with an introduction by O. J. Simpson. Still, *Psych IV* does provide some answers that Hitchcock neglected.

There are some other possible additions for the rest of this book's entries but there is no reason to let this get out of hand. Hopefully by now you will have broken into discussion groups. Discussion leaders should remember that not everyone works at the same speed. Indeed, some people never even get up to speed. Still, the goal of this book (besides every writer's pipe dream of making mega-bucks – I'm not holding my breath) is to have some fun with the invisible fourth wall which separates the film characters from all us voyeurs.

The movies provide us with fascinating stars, from *The Wizard Of Oz*'s Judy Garland, to *Bringing Up Baby*'s Wizard of Odd Katharine Hepburn. We live vicariously through their characters, except maybe Perkins' Norman Bates. And whether that's healthy or not (as in, get a life [2]) it is good to occasionally step back and have fun with all that time we spend in the dark. Spoofing allows more laughter and maybe a modicum of movie insight about the films we like. If nothing else, it gives you something to think about between your next double-feature . . . and I hope we won't have to have this conversation again.

---

[2] It's even worse for someone like the author, who decided early on not to get a life and now spends his time teaching film history to apprentice voyeurs.

Printed in the United States
4998